CRUNCHY DEEP FRIED PRAWNS (page 34)

BEEF IN A NEST (page 96)

PINEAPPLE FRIED RICE (page 102)

STUFFED CRAB CLAWS (page 35)

PAPER WRAPPED CHICKEN (page 75)

GUM LOW WON TON (page 106)

CURRIED BEEF SKEWER (page 98)

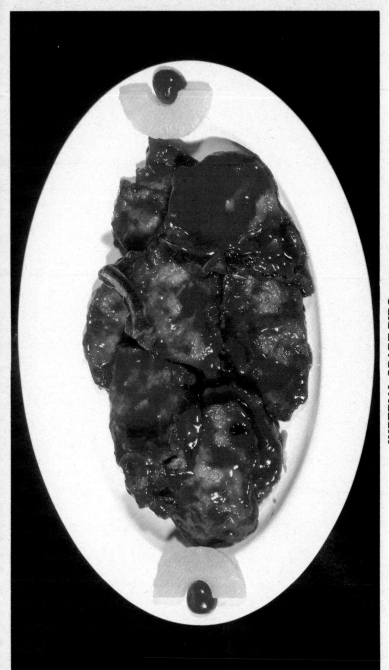

IMPERIAL SPARE RIBS (page 67)

WOK WITH YAN
TELEVISION COOKBOOK

by
STEPHEN YAN

Over 160 tested recipes used for the popular CBC National Chinese Cooking Show, "WOK WITH YAN" and restaurant cooking at Yan's Chinese Restaurant, 9948 Lougheed Highway, Burnaby, B.C., Canada.

1st Edition 1981

2nd Edition 1982

3rd Edition 1983

PUBLISHED BY:
YAN'S VARIETY COMPANY LIMITED
P.O. Box 227
Port Coquitlam, B.C., V3C 3V7
CANADA

WOK AN HONOUR!

ABOUT THE AUTHOR

Born and raised in Hong Kong, Mr. Stephen Yan received his training and practice in authentic Chinese cooking since the age of ten. He came to North America in 1963 and has taught thousands of students through his cooking classes, public demonstrations, radio and television shows.

Mr. Yan is:

- President of Yan's Variety Company Ltd., which manufactures Chinese cookware and condiments supplying hundreds of outlets throughout Canada.

- Owner of Yan's Gourmet Chinese Restaurant located in Burnaby, B.C., Canada.

- Host and Producer of "WOK WITH YAN", shown daily on the Canadian Broadcasting Corporation national network, cable networks in U.S.A., and internationally.

- Host of "Yan's Wokking" on the British Columbia Television Broadcasting System Ltd.

- Author of five "best seller" Chinese cookbooks.

- Member of Chaine Des Rotisseurs and American Chef Institute.

Mr. Yan's active participation in public appearances throughout Canada and the U.S.A., and his extensive travels throughout China, Hong Kong, South-east Asia and Australia have made him a popular celebrity.

American Chef Institute
American Hospitality Association

EDUCATION
PIONEER AWARD

PROUDLY PRESENTED TO

Stephen Yan's
Restaurant

in grateful recognition and appreciation for outstanding service in behalf of the American Chef Institute, the American Hospitality Association and the culinary profession in pioneering service and abiding interest to encourage the advancement and education of American youth in the culinary arts.

C.A.C.

FOREWORD

This outstanding Television Cookbook is primarily a collection of new recipes shown on the popular "WOK WITH YAN" television show. It contains over 160 recipes, with full colour photographic illustrations and a special section entitled "HOW TO" which provides basic hints and tips on effective ways to successful Chinese cooking. It highlights various regional cooking from China focusing on the beauty of appearance, aroma and taste.

My association with North Americans since 1963 has enabled me to recognize their cooking needs and present them in this book with easy-to-follow recipes to ensure cooking is easy, enjoyable and exciting. All the recipes have passed the test of my severest critics: my television viewers, my restaurant customers and my cooking school students.

The purpose of this book supports my lifetime ambition to share delicious Chinese cooking with all my friends. It is a tasteful way to bridge the two great cultures to a better understanding and friendship.

It is my sincere hope to inspire each reader to promote good cooking and bring the enjoyment back to home life to be shared between family and friends. I feel good cooking can be an attractive nucleus to bring people together as we have done in our television shows. As said in China:

"A country exists with people, and people live on food."

Happy Woking!

Stephen Yan,
Vancouver, B.C., Canada
1981

BASIC UTENSILS FOR CHINESE COOKING

THE WOK is a concave metal pan, looks like a salad bowl. Its uses are endless, e.g. to stir fry, deep fry, braise, saute, stew, blanch and steam.

Shape:

(1) **Flat bottom** — has the advantage of sitting directly on top of electric burner and receives quicker heat conduction, especially good for smooth top stove. It requires more oil in cooking, burns food more easily, can not be tilted to side for cooking and hinders tossing of ingredients.

(2) **Round bottom** — requires less oil in cooking, has no corners to hinder turning or removal of food. It conducts heat more effectively. Needs a metal collar or base. Can be used for gas, electric or open fire cooking. Round bottom type is recommended. Originally designed by the Chinese thousands of years ago and still used today.

Size:

14 inch diameter is sufficient for cooking for 2 · 15 people.

Material:

Steel Wok — requires scrubbing and seasoning depending on the type of steel. Complete dryness after use must be ensured, otherwise it gets rusty rapidly.

Stainless Steel with Copper Bottom — very ideal and popular in average western kitchen as it never requires seasoning or gets rusty. Usually dishwasher proof and requires minimal amount of care.

Teflon Coated Wok — teflon coating hinders conduction of heat and is not used in average Chinese kitchen.

Electric Wok — not recommended because:
(1) Poor heat conduction due to the teflon coating;
(2) less flexible, can not be used on gas range, nor be tilted to do cooking;
(3) very expensive but less efficient;
(4) normally not used by oriental people.
(5) cannot stir fry with metal spatula as it will damage the teflon coating.

The Wok Base:

For electric stove — usually made with steel. It sits in the inside diameter of the electric burner and should not cover the chrome ring of the stove as the reflection of high heat will discolour the enamel of the stove. It should have 3 holes on the side to prevent over heating (see picture).

For gas stove — it is larger, higher and has more holes so that air can get in to assist the fire combustion (see picture).

The Wok Cover: a 13 inch cover fits a 14 inch wok. The wok cover helps to build up steam pressure particularly in vegetable cooking and meat stewing. The wok cover I designed has a multiple purpose as it can be used as a holding tray when inverted as well as a wok cover (see picture).

Cleaver: a very versatile and indispensible item. Its broad blade allows uniform cutting and thin slicing. It can also be used for shredding, dicing, peeling, slivering and skinning garlic cloves. It replaces a whole battery of knives used in an average western kitchen. Carbon steel rusts easily if not properly dried. Stainless steel are available.

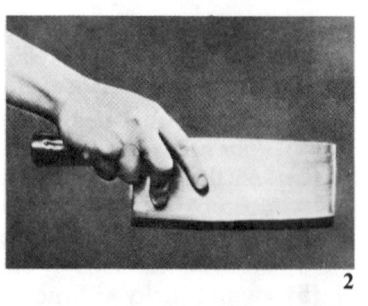

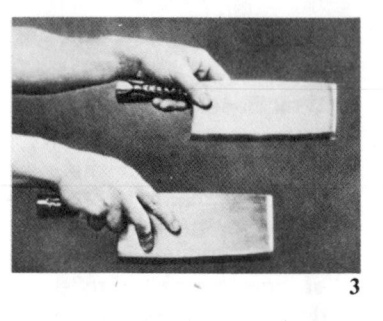

Chinese Spatula: has a curved blade to fit a round Chinese wok. It is used for stirring and turning ingredients in wok to prevent burning.

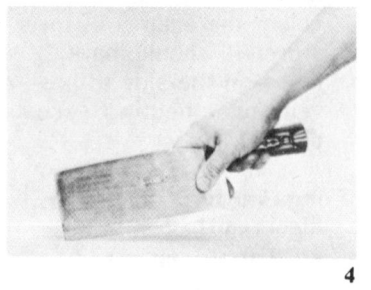

8

BASIC INGREDIENTS FREQUENTLY USED IN CHINESE COOKING

Chinese cooking ingredients and utensils are available at YAN'S VARIETY COMPANY LTD., Post Office Box 227, Port Coquitlam, British Columbia, CANADA. Phone number 941-3233. Mail orders are accepted.

CHINESE GOURMET POWDER
Monosodium Glutamate (M.S.G.), made from cereals in China. Salt-like in appearance, has the virtue of bringing out and accentuating the flavour of any food with which it is employed.

CHINESE COOKING WINE
Special rice wine is effective in the marination of meats particularly in chicken. It is a meat tenderizer and flavour promoter.

DRIED MUSHROOMS
Black mushrooms are sold in dried state. Can be kept for a long time. Soaking in hot water for half an hour is necessary before use. Produce exotic flavour and smell in Chinese dishes.

GINGER
Knotty knobs of ginger roots are used frequently in Chinese cooking. It can be kept for weeks in a cool dry place. Refrigeration is not required. It should be peeled before use. Powdered ginger can be used as a substitute.

FIVE SPICE POWDER
A special mixture of 5 spices from China. Very strong in flavour and is an appetizing agent in cooking. Used mainly for stewing and barbequing meats.

HOI SIN SAUCE
A highly seasoned sauce, brown in colour, made from Chinese pumpkin, sugar, spices and soy sauce. Used in barbecuing, steaming and stir frying.

OYSTER SAUCE
A thick brown sauce with no fishy taste. Excellent for seasoning vegetables, meats and noodles.

YAN'S WONDER POWDER

Very fine white tapioca powder similar to cornstarch but more starchy and turns any food from a dull colour to an attractive glossy look. Used frequently to thicken sauce or gravy. It has a mild tenderizing affect on meats, therefore it is used in various marinations.

SESAME SEED OIL

Reddish-brown oil has the effect to add flavour to any kind of dish. To be used in terms of drops only. It has a strong smell of sesame, sold in small bottles and does not require refrigeration.

SALTED BLACK BEANS

Soft, fermented black beans sold in plastic bags. An ingredient in Chinese cooking that produces an exotic and delicious flavour. They can be kept indefinitely in a covered container if stored in a refrigerator.

LIGHT SOY SAUCE

An important item in Chinese cooking as salt is to American cookery. It adds distinctive flavour in marination. Light brown in colour, salty but does not stain vegetables in cooking.

DARK SOY SAUCE

Usually found in Chinese specialty shops. Dark brown in colour, has a sweet taste and is used frequently for stewing and food colouring in Chinese cooking.

CHINESE PEANUT OIL

Pure 100 per cent peanut with a delightful smell and flavour to make Chinese cooking more delicious and appetizing.

YAN'S ALMIGHTY POWDER

An all purpose battermix powder prepared with egg white powder, bread crumbs, flour, starch and salt. Just add equal amounts of water and powder, then mix into a smooth consistency. Excellent for all types of deep frying.

TABLE OF CONTENTS

SEAFOOD:

VEGETABLES:

SOUPS:

PORK:

CHICKEN:

BEEF:

RICE AND NOODLE:

MISCELLANEOUS:

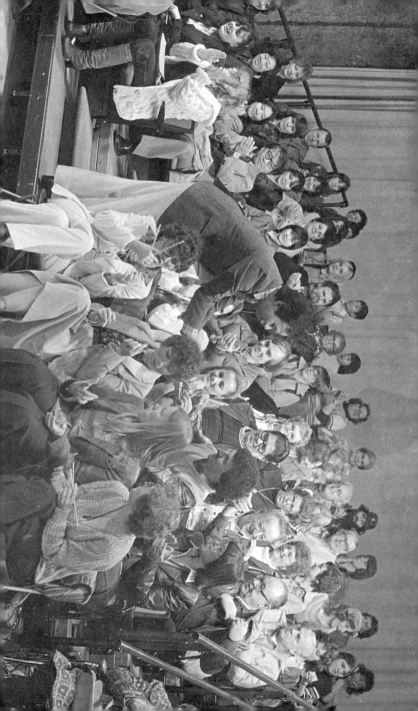

TIPS AND HINTS FOR SUCCESSFUL CHINESE COOKING

PLANNING:

—Consider your own ability and do not plan for more dishes than you can handle.

—Choose most dishes that can be cooked ahead of time and pick only one last minute dish for your menu.

PREPARATION:

—Check the ingredient list for completeness. Assemble all the ingredients in one place, preferably on a large tray near the stove for cooking.

—Preparation takes up more time than the actual cooking. Allow time to prepare all ingredients.

—Washing and cutting should be done ahead of time.

—Most ingredients are cut to uniform bite size, shape and thickness. Cutting diagonally increases the exposure to heat and ensures better cooking.

—Meats should be thinly sliced across the grain to give more tenderness.

—Oil and seasoning ingredients should be readily accessible on counter.

—Marination should be done ahead of time.

COOKING:

—Study and understand the procedure before any cooking.

—The wok must be hot and use high heat to do cooking unless specified.

—Prepare rice or noodle dishes first; cook vegetables dishes last.

—When food is being cooked with a lid, DO NOT take lid off until time is up. If steam pressure is lost, the food will take longer time to cook.

—Cook quickly, serve immediately.

MENU PLANNING

Samples of menus are listed for various occasions and for number of people served. Assuming 4 to 6 people in a family, a sufficient menu should consist of 1 soup, 1 rice, 1 dish with vegetables and 3 meat dishes. For every addition of 2 persons, another meat dish should be added.

The contrast and diversity of dishes must be considered. When one is spicy, another one should be bland; if one is meaty, the other should be more vegetables; when there is 1 dish of chicken, the other should consist of other kinds of meat to avoid duplication; when filling dish like steamed rice is planned, one should avoid another filling dish like chow mein or fried rice.

Be honest with your own ability and do not plan several dishes for last minute cooking. It is always recommendable that only one last minute stir-fry dish per menu be considered and pick the rest that can be done ahead of time.

MENU SAMPLES

MENU FOR 4 PEOPLE:

Colourful Shrimp Soup   Pork with Baby Corn
Beef Rolls   Minced Beef Fried Rice
Sweet & Sour Drumsticks

MENU FOR 8 PEOPLE:

Westlake Beef Soup   Honey Beef
Three is Company   Stuffed Chicken Wings
Beef with Cashewnut   Buddhist Feast
Crunchy Deep Fried Prawns   Pork Chow Mein

MENU FOR BUFFET PARTY:
(more than 10 people)

Gum Low Wonton   Pork with Broccolli
Soy Sauce Chicken   Beef Stuffed Mushrooms
Crunchy Deep Fried Prawns   Minced Beef Fried Rice
Fruited Pork   Yan's Hot Noodles
Sesame Fish   Almond Cookies

HOW TO

HEAT WOK
1. Use high heat to heat up the wok.
2. Using a hot wok, add 2 Tbsp. of Chinese peanut oil in a swirling motion.
3. When oil is hot, start cooking.

STIR FRY
1. Use high heat and heat wok until it is hot.
2. Add 2 Tbsp. Chinese Peanut Oil in a swirling motion and add ½ tsp. salt. When oil is hot, add all vegetables and stir.
3. Add 2 - 3 Tbsp. of water & seasoning (or chicken broth) and cover with a lid. Cook at high heat until steam escapes from the edge of the lid.

DEEP FRY IN A WOK
1. Pour about 2 Cups Chinese Peanut Oil in wok.
2. Use high heat to start out — when the oil ripples and smokes, use a bamboo chop stick to test the temperature. If bubbles form around the chop stick, then the oil is hot enough for deep frying. If it is too hot (excessive smoke will shoot up) then add extra oil to cool it down before you begin to deep fry.

SEASON SPUN STEEL WOKS
A. 1. Scour the inside with S.O.S., soap and water for about 5 minutes. Rinse and dry well with paper towel.
   2. Smear oil on the inside surface.
   3. Heat over "high heat" until wok becomes discoloured. Tilt wok to get even seasoning. The discolouration is the sign of seasoning.
   4. After use, the wok should be washed immediately and dried by putting it back on the stove. The remaining heat will provide extra dryness.

B. Another method is:
   1. Wash the wok with S.O.S. pads, rinse and dry with paper towel;
   2. Oil the whole wok;
   3. Put in the oven at 450⁰ for 30 minutes. The whole wok will turn black. This discolouration indicates that the entire wok has been seasoned.

HOW TO

PREPARE POTATO BASKET

1. Use large potato, cut into thin slivers (i.e. shoe strings). Soak in water for 2 hours to remove excessive starch. Drain well and dry in towel for ½ hour. Place in bowl and sprinkle with 1 Tbsp. tapioca starch.

2. Dip 2 wire ladles in oil. Spread shoe string potatoes evenly inside one wire ladle. Place second wire ladle on potatoes and press 2 ladles together firmly.

3. Deep fry in 6 cups of oil until golden brown. Remove, carefully from wire ladle, drain and place on platter for later use.

MAKE WON TON OR EGG ROLL SKINS

This is a home made method for the paper thin Won Ton Skin. It is very therapeutic if you have the time. This skin can be used to wrap up won tons, dim sum or even egg rolls.

INGREDIENTS:

1 Egg, beaten
2 C. flour
¼ tsp. salt
¾ C. water

METHOD:

1. Sift flour and salt, then mix with the egg and water to form dough.
2. Roll out on board until paper thin. Use a sharp cleaver and trim edges to 16" squares. Cut into 4" squares.

If Won Ton Skin is not being used right away, dust surface with dry flour before stacking them. Cover with a moist towel to prevent dryness. Should be stored in refrigerator.

If the skin is being used for egg rolls, cut into larger squares.

MAKE STARCH SOLUTION:

1. Dissolve 1 Tbsp. Wonder Powder in ¼ C. water.
2. For shiny affect, add a few drops of Sesame Seed Oil.
3. Stir well before using.

MAKE RICE CAKE FOR SIZZLING SOUP

1. Cook rice and spread about ½ inch thick on greased cookie sheet, press into an even layer.
2. Bake in oven at medium heat until rice is very dry (about 1-2 hrs.).
3. When cool, break into 2" squares and store in an air-tight container. (Can be kept for up to 3 months).

COOK PERFECT STEAMED RICE

INGREDIENTS: (Yields 3 C.)
1 C. long grain rice
1½ C. water

When more rice is required, simply add same proportional amount of water.

METHOD:

1) Wash rice by rubbing it between palm of hands. Drain all water.
2) Add correct amount of water to rice. Any temperature of water can be used. DO **NOT** salt or butter to cook rice as it will destroy the sweet flavour of good steamed rice.
3) Cook rice in a saucepan over high heat, **UNCOVERED**, until tiny holes or craters form over the surface of the rice. Switch to low heat and cover tightly with a lid. Simmer the rice for 15-20 mins. **DO NOT TAKE LID OFF** until time is up. This is the most critical time, as the rice is steam-cooked under pressure. When done, stir and serve hot.

Note: Left over steamed rice can be saved and kept in refrigerator until sufficient to make fried rice. As a matter of fact, freshly cooked rice is too soft and not suitable for fried rice. Try to cook the rice ahead of time if you need cooked rice for frying. Also fluff up the cooked rice before storing. This makes it easier to handle when frying and improves the final result giving it a more professional appearance.

MAKE CHICKEN BROTH

Use large soup pot, put in the following ingredients:
3 lbs. boney chicken pieces (necks, backs or wings)
2 quarts, water
4 slices ginger
2 green onion, cut to 2" lengths.

METHOD:

1. Bring water to a boil. Skim off foam that rises to the top.
2. Reduce heat to low and simmer for 2 hours.
3. Add salt to taste.

Makes about 1 quart.

HOW TO

GROW BEAN SPROUTS SUCCESSFULLY AT HOME

Mung beans (as they are called in China), or green beans are used for sprouting bean sprouts. They are very easy to grow but do require very careful timing.

INGREDIENTS:

1 C. Mung Beans
Clay Flower Pot, with drains at the bottom
Cheesecloth

METHOD:

1. Soak mung beans in warm water over night.
2. Line the bottom of a clay flower pot with 2 layers of cheesecloth.
3. Next morning, drain water off beans.
4. Place soaked mung beans into pot and run under cold water.
5. Cover the beans with a layer of cheesecloth or light towel.
6. Place in a dark room, at room temperature and water (on top of the cheesecloth) about three times daily.
7. For better results, you can use a plastic bag filled with water and tie the end. Place this on top of the cheesecloth to act as a weight. The sprouts will then come out faster.
8. After about five days, take the bean sprouts out and rinse off the green skin. They are then ready for use.

PREPARE A CRAB FOR COOKING

1. Pull the "apron" off the underside of the crab with fingers.
2. Lift the shell off the body of the crab.
3. Use cleaver and chop the claw at the joint area.
4. Use the back of cleaver to crack claws.
5. Divide the body into 8-10 sections, leaving a leg on each section.
6. Remove the gills and wash the body.

HOW TO

USE CHOP STICKS
THE PROPER WAY

1) Hold one chop stick in the middle using your thumb, index and middle finger. Move it up and down, as if holding a "pencil". This becomes the moving stick. (See figure 1)

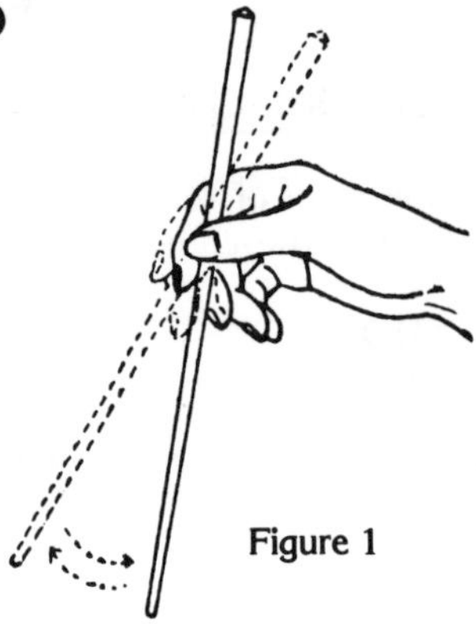

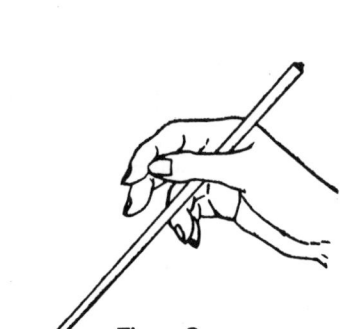

Figure 1

2) Rest another chop stick on the joint of your thumb and index finger. This chop stick SHOULD NOT MOVE at all. (See figure 2.)

Figure 2

3) Put the two sticks together and move the "pencil" one up and down making sure the ends are together otherwise you will not pick up anything. (See figure 3.)

REMEMBER — MOVE
THE TOP STICK ONLY.

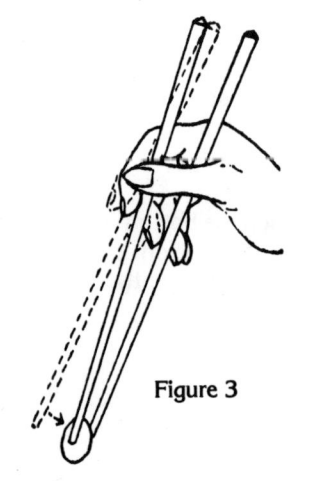

Figure 3

25

HOW TO

DEBONE CHICKEN BREAST — THE YAN'S WAY

A whole piece of fresh chicken breast without any breakage at the top part is recommended for easy performance.

METHOD:

1. Find the small opening at the bottom part of the rib cage and insert your index finger all the way to the top.

2. Move the index finger forward to expose the ribs.

3. Dig your finger into the muscle to feel for the inside muscle. Then move up and down to expose the inside muscle which can be seen in longitudinal position.

4. Use your index finger to elevate the inside muscle from the cartilage and the breast bone. Once the top white tendon is exposed, grip it with fingers and pull gently downward. The inside muscle is removed and can be put aside.
Repeat steps 1 to 4 on the other side of the breast.

5. Hang on the bone part upward. Insert both thumbs into the transparent membrane. Exert thumbs in opposite directions to create a breakage at the bone area.

6. Slide the bottom thumb towards the tip of the cartilage to break off the bottom part. Break off the top part and then remove wish-bone gently.

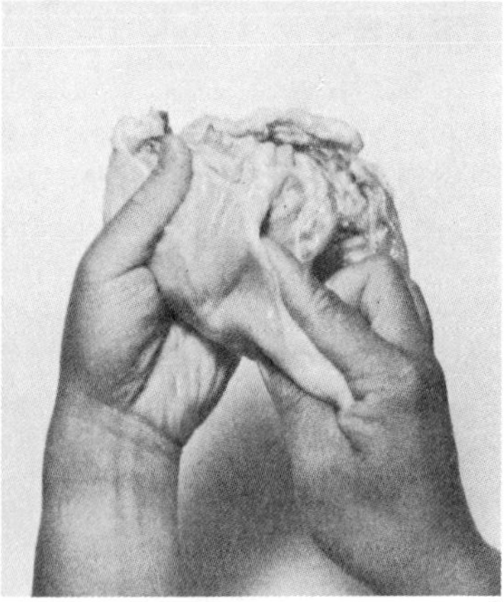
1

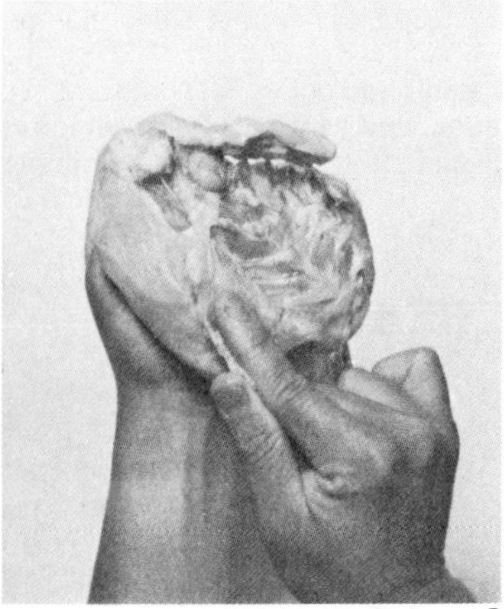
2

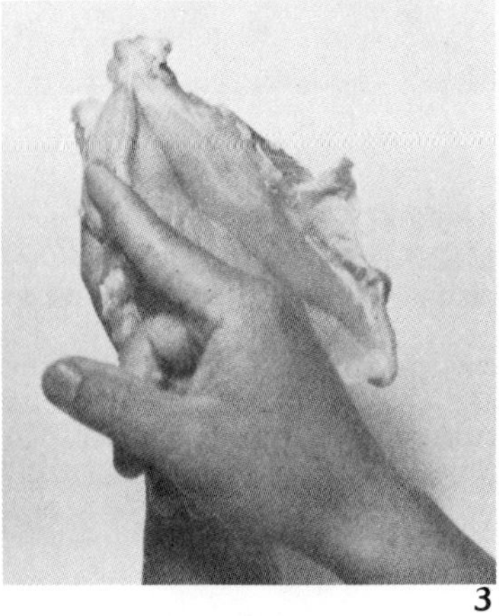
3

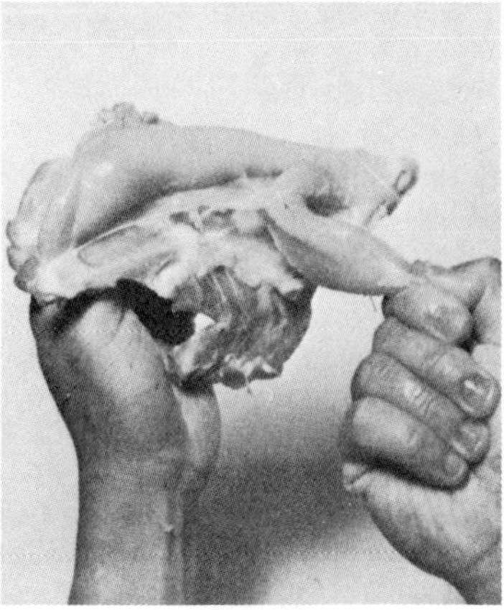
4

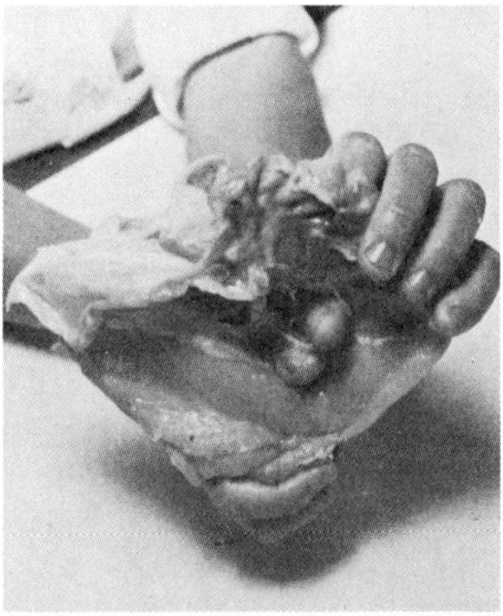
5

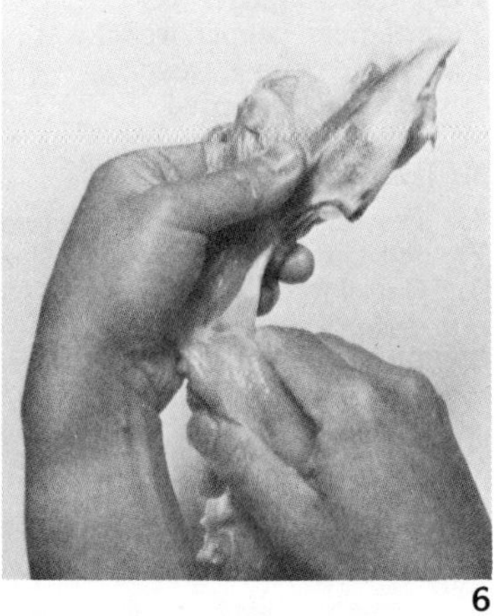
6

HOI SIN CRABS

INGREDIENTS:

2 lb. crab. whole, uncooked
3 Tbsp. YAN'S Wonder Powder
½ tsp. salt
1 tsp. minced garlic
1 Tbsp. minced ginger
1 small red pepper, wedged
1 small onion, wedged
1 small green pepper, wedged

SAUCE:

3 Tbsp. hoi sin sauce
1 Tbsp. light soy sauce
1 Tbsp. dark soy sauce
dash pepper
drops sesame seed oil
1 Tbsp. Chinese cooking wine
1 tsp. sugar
1 Tbsp. Wonder Powder

METHOD:

1) Prepare crab for cooking*. (**refer HOW TO p. 24**)
2) With the side of cleaver, crack the legs and claws to allow the sauce to go into the crab meat.
3) Put crab in wok lid and dust with YAN'S Wonder Powder.
4) Heat up 4 C. of peanut oil in wok. Deep fry crab until color changes. Remove from oil and drain.
5) HEAT WOK* put in minced ginger, garlic and onion. Add crab and ¼ C. water, saute for 1 minute. Add sauce, cover with a lid and cook for a couple of minutes. Add vegetables and stir mix for one more minute.

*refer HOW TO p. 21

CRAB IN BLACK BEAN SAUCE

INGREDIENTS:

1 fresh uncooked crab
  (2 lb. size, cracked & cut into
  pieces)
2 Tbsp. salted black beans
  (rinsed)
1 Tbsp. minced garlic
1 tsp. minced ginger
1 small green pepper, wedged
1 small red pepper, wedged
½ small onion, wedged

SAUCE:

1 Tbsp. dark soy sauce
pinch sugar
2 Tbsp. light soy sauce
drops sesame seed oil
1 Tbsp. Chinese cooking wine
1 Tbsp. Wonder Powder

METHOD:

1) Prepare crab for cooking*. (**refer HOW TO p. 24**).
2) Put crab in large bowl and dust with 2 Tbsp. Wonder Powder.
3) Heat 4 C. oil in wok and deep fry crab until it changes color. Remove and drain.
4) Clean and HEAT WOK*. Add garlic, ginger and salted black beans. Saute for 1 minute. Add crab, ½ tsp. Chinese cooking wine and ¼ C. water. STIR FRY* for 3 minutes. Add onion, pepper, and sauce, cook until boil.

*refer HOW TO p. 21.

SHRIMP IN BLACK BEAN SAUCE

INGREDIENTS:

1 lb. shrimp, fresh, uncooked
   shelled and deveined
2 Tbsp. salted black beans, rinsed
1 tsp. minced garlic
½ tsp. minced ginger
1 small onion, wedged
1 small red pepper, wedged
1 small green pepper, wedged

SAUCE:

1 Tbsp. dark soy sauce
1 Tbsp. light soy sauce
1 tsp. sugar
¼ tsp. gourmet powder
drops sesame seed oil
1 Tbsp. Wonder Powder
¼ C. water

SEAFOODS

METHOD:

1) HEAT WOK*, add ginger, garlic, onion, peppers and salted black beans. Saute for 30 seconds.
2) Add shrimp and stir until shrimp curl up and change color.
3) Add sauce and bring to a boil.

*refer HOW TO p. 21

SCALLOPS WITH BABY CORN

INGREDIENTS:

1 lb. scallops, cut in half
1 can baby corn
1 tsp. minced ginger
½ tsp. minced garlic
2 green onions, cut to 2" lengths

SAUCE:

1 tsp. salt
1 tsp. sugar
¼ tsp. gourmet powder
drops sesame seed oil
dash pepper
1 Tbsp. Wonder Powder
¼ C. water

METHOD:

1) Marinate scallops with 1 Tbsp. Wonder Powder, ½ tsp. salt, 1 Tbsp. Chinese cooking wine and drops of sesame seed oil.
2) HEAT WOK*, brown green onion, garlic and ginger; put in scallops, saute for 2 minutes. Remove and set aside.
3) Add sauce and bring to a boil. Serve hot.

*refer HOW TO p. 21

SESAME FISH

INGREDIENTS:

1 lb. fish filet, cut to
  1 x 2½" pcs.
20 slices bacon, 1 x 2½"
1 Tbsp. green onion, finely chopped
½ tsp. ginger, minced
½ tsp. garlic, minced

2 eggs, beaten
¼ C. YAN'S Almighty Powder
½ C. sesame seeds

METHOD:

1) Marinate fish with 1 tsp. salt, 1 tsp. sugar, ½ tsp. 5 spice powder, 1 Tbsp. cooking wine and ½ tsp. sesame seed oil.
2) Use beaten egg to stick each slice of fish with 1 pc. of bacon. Then dip the combined fish and bacon into beaten egg and roll on the mixture of YAN'S Almighty Powder and sesame seeds. Set aside.
3) HEAT WOK* and smear 1 Tbsp. oil. Pan fry the fish until light brown. Remove and set aside.
4) DEEP FRY* fish at medium/high heat until golden brown. Drain oil and transfer to a platter garnished with lettuce leaves.

*refer HOW TO p. 21

PRAWNS BOUQUET

INGREDIENTS:

12 prawns, (size 15-20)
24 broccoli flowerets
1 green onion, minced
½ tsp. minced ginger
½ tsp. minced garlic
½ tsp. baking soda

SAUCE:

½ tsp. salt
½ tsp. sugar
¼ tsp. gourmet powder
1 tsp. Chinese cooking wine
drops of sesame seed oil
dash pepper
1½ Tbsp. Wonder Powder
½ C. water

METHOD:

1) Shell prawn body but leave the tail on. Cut prawn back lengthwise and devein, to flatten prawns body. Pierce a slit in the upper part of the body and introduce the tail through the slit so that the prawn can stand by itself.
2) Marinate prawns with ½ tsp. salt, 1 tsp. Wonder Powder, ½ tsp. sesame oil and 1 Tbsp. peanut oil.
3) Blanch broccoli flowerets in boiling water with 1 tsp. salt, 1 tsp. sugar, 1 Tbsp. oil and ½ tsp. baking soda. Drain and display around a platter.
4) Blanch prawns in boiling water with 1 Tbsp. peanut oil until done. Drain and display in the middle of a platter.
5) HEAT WOK*, brown ginger, garlic and green onions. Add sauce and bring to a boil. Pour over prawns and broccoli.

*refer HOW TO p. 21

PRAWNS WITH BROCCOLI (page 48)

CRAB IN BLACK BEAN SAUCE (page 28)

**STEPHEN'S RESTAURANT AT 9948 LOUGHEED HWY.
BURNABY, B.C., CANADA — TEL: (604) 421-8888**

INSIDE YAN'S CHINESE RESTAURANT

BUTTERED LOBSTER (page 38)

MUSHROOMS IN A NEST (page 54)

BUTTERFLY PRAWNS (page 49)

PINEAPPLE FISH BALLS (page 33)

SHRIMP DUMPLINGS (page 110)

SHRIMP WITH CASHEW NUTS (page 43)

WOK'S NEW PUSSY CAT

WOK BEFORE YOU RUN

PINEAPPLE HONEY CHICKEN BALLS (page 81)

HONEYMOON FRIED RICE (page 101)

HAM FRIED RICE (page 103)

PRAWNS AND PEAS (page 33)

MUSHROOMS WITH CRAB MEAT

INGREDIENTS:

1 C. straw mushrooms
1 ½ C. fresh mushrooms
½ C. crab meat
2 egg whites
1 green onion cut to 1" lengths
1 tsp. minced ginger
½ tsp. minced garlic

SAUCE:

½ tsp. salt
½ tsp. sugar
¼ tsp. gourmet powder
1 tsp. Chinese cooking wine
drops sesame seed oil
dash pepper
2 Tbsp. Wonder Powder
½ C. water

METHOD:

1) STIR FRY* mushrooms, drain and arrange on platter.
2) HEAT WOK*, brown green onion, ginger; put in crab meat and saute for few seconds. Add sauce and bring to a boil. Stir in egg white and pour over mushrooms to serve.

*refer HOW TO p. 21

SATAY PRAWN ON A SKEWER

INGREDIENTS:

24 fresh prawns, shelled and
   deveined
2 Tbsp. satay powder

½ cucumber, sliced
6 bamboo skewers

SEASONING:

1 tsp. salt
1 tsp. sugar
¼ tsp. gourmet powder
1 tsp. Chinese cooking wine
drops of sesame seed oil
1 tsp. Wonder Powder
2 Tbsp. water

METHOD:

1) Marinate prawn with satay powder and all seasoning. Arrange prawns on skewers.
2) Heat oil, DEEP FRY* prawns until it changes color to red. Drain oil and arrange on a platter garnished with cucumber slices.

*refer HOW TO p. 21

FRUITED SCALLOPS

INGREDIENTS:
12 oz. fresh scallops, cut in half
1/3 C. canned apricot, cut in 1" cubes
1/3 C. pineapple chunks
1/3 C frozen snow peas, thawed
   cut in half
½ tsp. garlic, minced
½ tsp. ginger, minced
1 green onion, cut to 1" length

SAUCE:
½ tsp. salt
1/3 C. apricot syrup
1 Tbsp. lemon juice
1 Tbsp. Wonder Powder
2 Tbsp. water

SEAFOODS

METHOD:

1) Marinate scallops with 1 tsp. Wonder Powder, ½ tsp. salt, 1 tsp. cooking wine, and drops of sesame see oil.

2) HEAT WOK*, brown green onion, garlic and ginger; put in scallops and snow peas and saute for 5 minutes. Add all canned fruits and sauce, cook until boil. Remove to a platter.

*refer HOW TO p. 21

STIR FRIED FISH

INGREDIENTS:
1 lb. fish filet, sliced
1 C. celery, sliced
½ C. carrot, sliced
½ tsp. minced garlic
½ tsp. minced ginger
1 stalk green onion, cut to
   1" length

SAUCE:
½ tsp. salt
½ tsp. sugar
1 tsp. Chinese cooking wine
1 Tbsp. oyster sauce
drop of sesame seed oil
dash of pepper
1 Tbsp. Wonder Powder
¼ C. water

METHOD:

1) Marinate fish with 1 Tbsp. Wonder Powder, 2 Tbsp. light soy, 1 Tbsp. cooking wine, and drops of sesame seed oil.

2) HEAT WOK*, brown green onion, garlic and ginger; put in fish and saute until fish changes color. Remove and set aside.

3) With same wok, add 1 Tbsp. peanut oil. STIR FRY* vegetables; return fish to wok. Add sauce and cook until boil. Serve hot.

*refer HOW TO p. 21

PRAWNS AND PEAS

INGREDIENTS:

1 lb. prawns, shelled
   and deveined
1 C. snow peas or green peas
1 small red pepper, wedged
1 small green pepper, wedged
1 small onion, wedged
2 stalks, green onion, cut to
   2" lengths
½ tsp. minced ginger
¼ tsp. minced garlic

SAUCE:

½ tsp. salt
¼ tsp. gourmet powder
1 tsp. sugar
drops of sesame seed oil
1 Tbsp. Wonder Powder
¼ C. water

SEAFOODS

METHOD:

1) Marinate prawns with ½ tsp. salt, 1 tsp. Wonder Powder.
2) HEAT WOK*, brown ginger, garlic, put in prawns, saute for 2 min. at light heat and sprinkle with 1 Tbsp. Chinese cooking wine. Remove and set aside.
3) HEAT WOK*, STIR FRY* vegetables, return prawns to wok, add sauce and cook until boil.

*refer HOW TO p. 21

PINEAPPLE FISH BALLS

INGREDIENTS:

10 oz. fish fillet, cubed
½ onion, wedged
1 green onion, cut to
   1" lengths
1 tsp. minced garlic
1 tsp. minced ginger
½ C. YAN's Almighty Powder
1 egg

SAUCE:

½ C. pineapple tidbits
3 Tbsp. sugar
3 Tbsp. tomato ketchup
1 Tbsp. vinegar
1 Tbsp. dark soy sauce
1½ Tbsp. Wonder Powder
½ C. water

METHOD:

1) Marinate fish fillet with ½ tsp. salt, drops of sesame seed oil and egg.
2) Heat 2 C. of peanut oil in wok. Roll fish fillet in YAN's Almighty Powder. Deep fry until golden brown. Drain and set aside.
3) Clean and HEAT WOK*. Saute onion, ginger and garlic. Add sauce and bring to a boil. Return deep fried fish. Mix well and serve.

*refer HOW TO p. 21

BREADED ALMOND FISH

INGREDIENTS:

1 lb. fish filet, sliced to
    ¼" thickness
¼ tsp. salt
dash pepper
¼ tsp. gourmet powder
1 C. YAN'S Almighty Powder
    (dissolved in 1 C. water & drops
    of oil)
drops sesame seed oil

MIXTURE OF ALMOND POWDER:

2 Tbsp. bread crumbs
4 Tbsp. ground roasted almonds
½ tsp. salt
½ tsp. sugar

METHOD:

1) Wash and dry fish filet on absorbent paper towel. Sprinkle with salt, pepper and gourmet powder.
2) Coat fish with battermix and then into hot oil, DEEP FRY* until golden brown. When finished, drain and sprinkle with almond powder. Serve hot.

*refer HOW TO p. 21

CRUNCHY DEEP FRIED PRAWNS

INGREDIENTS:

12 prawns, shelled & deveined but
    leave tail on
½ C. rice vermicelli, chopped fine
¾ C. YAN'S Almighty Powder
    (dissolved in ¾ C. water)
¼ tsp. Chinese 5 spice powder
Romain lettuce leaves for garnishing
12 bamboo skewers

SAUCE:

½ tsp. tobasco sauce
4 Tbsp. pineapple juice
2 Tbsp. honey
2 Tbsp. vinegar
1 Tbsp. Wonder Powder
½ C. water

METHOD:

1) Marinate prawns with 1 tsp. salt, ¼ tsp. 5 spice powder and drops of sesame oil. Pierce bamboo skewer from prawns tail to front part.
2) Coat prawns with batter, then roll on chopped rice vermicelli and DEEP FRY* at medium/high heat until golden brown. Transfer to a platter garnished with lettuce leaves.
3) HEAT WOK*, add sauce and bring to a boil. Transfer to a sauce bowl for dipping. (May use YAN'S Plum Sauce as substitute).

*refer HOW TO p. 21

34

STUFFED CRAB CLAWS

INGREDIENTS:

8 crab claws
1 lb. raw shrimp, shelled and
    deveined
1 tsp. minced ginger
1 tsp. minced green onion
3 oz. fresh pork fat, blanched
    and minced
1 egg white

SEASONING:

1 tsp. salt
1 tsp. sugar
¼ tsp. gourmet powder
drops of sesame seed oil
dash pepper
2 Tbsp. Wonder Powder
3 Tbsp. water

METHOD:

1) Use cleaver blade, smash raw shrimp.
2) In a bowl, mix all ingredients and seasoning except the crab claws. Stir and knead to make a condensed shrimp paste.
3) Using damp fingers, coat meaty part of the crab claw with shrimp paste to form oval shape — leave the shell end as a handle. Dust with Wonder Powder to prevent sticking to the holding tray.
4) Heat 4 C. of peanut oil in wok, DEEP FRY* with medium/high heat for 15 minutes. Stir occasionally. Drain and serve with worchestershire sauce.

*refer HOW TO p. 21

MID AUTUMN FESTIVAL PRAWNS

INGREDIENTS:

12 fresh prawns, shelled with tail
    remaining and deveined by slitting
    from back
12 slices bacon, 1 x 2"
2 eggs beaten
2 C. mashed potatoes
2 tsp. YAN'S Wonder Powder
½ C. bread crumbs
¼ C. YAN'S Almighty Powder

SEASONING:

½ tsp. salt
½ tsp. sugar
drop of sesame seed oil
dash pepper
2 Tbsp. YAN'S Wonder Powder

METHOD:

1) Flatten prawn and lay one slice bacon on top. Coat with YAN'S Wonder Powder. Wrap entirely with mashed potato (4-6 Tbsp) into a rectangular shape. Coat with bread crumbs.
2) DEEP FRY* with medium/high heat until golden brown.

*refer HOW TO page 21

CRAB MEAT WITH VEGETABLES

INGREDIENTS:

½ C. frozen crab meat, thawed
3 C. swiss chard, cut 2" lengths
1 Tbsp. green onion, chopped fine
1 tsp. minced ginger
½ tsp. minced garlic
1 egg white

SAUCE:

¹/₃ C. water
½ tsp. salt
½ tsp. sugar
¼ tsp. gourmet powder
1 tsp. Chinese cooking wine
drops of sesame seed oil
dash pepper
1 ½ Tbsp. Wonder Powder

METHOD:

1) HEAT WOK*, STIR FRY*, vegetables. Drain and arrange on a platter.
2) HEAT WOK*, brown green onion, ginger and garlic, saute crab meat for ½ minute. Add sauce and cook until boiling, stir in egg white and pour over vegetables to serve.

*refer HOW TO p. 21

FISH WITH CORN SAUCE

INGREDIENTS:

10 oz. fish filet, sliced
¾ C. YAN'S Almighty Powder
   dissolved in ¾ C. water

SAUCE:

½ tsp. salt
¼ tsp. gourmet powder
1 Tbsp. Chinese cooking wine
drops of sesame seed oil
dash pepper
¹/₃ C. water
1 Tbsp. Wonder Powder
½ C. creamed corn

METHOD:

1) Marinate fish with ½ tsp. salt and drops of sesame seed oil.
2) Heat peanut oil in wok, coat fish with batter and DEEP FRY* at medium/high heat until golden brown. Drain and transfer to a platter.
3) HEAT WOK*, add sauce and bring to a boil, pour over fish.

*refer HOW TO p. 21

DEEP FRIED FISH ROLLS

INGREDIENTS:

2 large fish filet cut to 4"x2" pcs.
12 pcs. cooked ham cut to 4"x2" pcs.
2 green onions, minced
½ tsp. garlic, minced
12 wooden cocktail sticks

¾ C. YAN'S Almighty Powder
   (dissolved in ¾ C. water)
½ C. walnuts, ground
1 C. watercress

METHOD:

1) Marinate fish with ½ tsp. salt, ½ tsp. sugar, 1 Tbsp. cooking wine and drops sesame seed oil.
2) Put 1 piece of fish on top of ham, roll and secure with cocktail stick.
3) Coat fish with batter then roll on ground walnuts and DEEP FRY* with medium heat to golden brown. Transfer to a platter garnished with watercress.

*refer HOW TO p. 21

FISH BALLS

INGREDIENTS:

1 C. fish filet, mashed
¼ C. minced pork
4 slices bread, cut to ⅛" cubes

SEASONING:

¼ tsp. salt
dash pepper
1 Tbsp. YAN'S Wonder Powder
1 egg white
1 tsp. sugar
drops of sesame seed oil

METHOD:

1) Mix fish and pork with the seasonings, stir mixture well until firm. Form into small balls and coat with the bread cubes.
2) Heat up oil in wok, DEEP FRY* with medium/high heat to golden brown. Drain oil and serve with worcestershire sauce.

*refer HOW TO p. 21

HOT & SOUR PRAWNS

SEAFOODS

INGREDIENTS:

1 lb. raw prawns, med. size
shelled and deveined
2 stalks celery, diced
½ tsp. minced garlic
1 tsp. minced ginger
½ C. bamboo shoots, sliced
2 green onions, chopped
1 Tbsp. Wonder Powder

SAUCE:

1 tsp. tobasco sauce
2 tsp. vinegar
2 Tbsp. dark soy sauce
6 tsp. sugar
1 tsp. Chinese cooking wine
drops of sesame seed oil
dash pepper
1 Tbsp. Wonder Powder
¼ C. water

METHOD:

1) Marinate prawns with 1 tsp. salt, 1 tsp. sugar, 1 Tbsp. Wonder Powder.
2) HEAT WOK*, brown garlic, ginger and onion. Put in prawns and saute until color changes. Remove and set aside.
3) Use same wok, put in all vegetables and STIR FRY*. Return prawns to wok, add sauce and bring to a boil.

*refer HOW TO p. 21

BUTTERED LOBSTER

INGREDIENTS:

2 lbs. lobster, uncooked
3 Tbsp. YAN'S Wonder Powder
1 tsp. salt
1 tsp. minced garlic
1 Tbsp. minced ginger
¼ C. butter

SAUCE:

dash pepper
1 Tbsp. Chinese cooking wine
½ tsp. sugar
½ tsp. salt
¼ tsp. gourmet powder
1 Tbsp. Wonder Powder
½ C. water

METHOD:

1) Cut off all legs with scissors. Cut off claws and sharp point of the head with cleaver. Remove head and divide the body into 4-5 sections. With blunt edge of cleaver, crack the claws.
2) Put lobster in wok lid and dust with YAN'S Wonder Powder and salt.
3) Heat up 4 cups of peanut oil in wok. DEEP FRY* lobster until color changes. Remove from oil and drain.
4) HEAT WOK* put in minced ginger, garlic and butter. Add lobster and saute for 1 minute. Add sauce, cover with a lid and cook for a couple of minutes. Stir mix.

*refer HOW TO p. 21

FISH IN LEMON SAUCE

INGREDIENTS:

1 lb. fish filet, cut to ¼"
   thickness
¼ tsp. salt
¼ tsp. 5 spice
dash pepper
1 Tbsp. YAN'S Wonder Powder
1 C. YAN'S Almighty Powder
   (dissolved in 1 C. water and
   drops of sesame seed oil)
¼ head lettuce, shredded

SAUCE:

6 slices of lemon
2 Tbsp. white vinegar
6 Tbsp. sugar
few drops lemon extract
few drops yellow food coloring
1 ½ Tbsp. Wonder Powder
½ C. water

METHOD:

1) Wash and dry the fish filets and sprinkle with salt, pepper and gourmet powder.
2) Dip fish into battermix, DEEP FRY* in hot oil until golden brown. Remove from oil and place on a plate bedded with shredded lettuce.
3) In a clean wok, cook sauce to a boil, then pour over fish.

*refer HOW TO p 21

SCALLOPS WITH MUSHROOMS

INGREDIENTS:

12 oz. fresh scallops
½ tsp. minced ginger
2 green onions, cut to 2" lengths
1 C. fresh mushrooms, cut in half
8 Chinese mushrooms, soaked for
   half hour and cut in half
¼ C. carrot slices
½ C. broccoli flowerets
½ tsp. salt

SAUCE:

1 Tbsp. Wonder Powder
1 Tbsp. oyster sauce
½ tsp. sugar
1 Tbsp. Chinese cooking wine
drops of sesame seed oil
¼ C. water

METHOD:

1) Marinate scallops with 1 Tbsp. of Wonder Powder, ½ tsp. salt and 1 Tbsp. Chinese cooking wine.
2) Blanch broccoli in boiling water with ¼ tsp. baking soda, ½ tsp. salt, and 2 Tbsp. oil; drain and display on platter.
3) HEAT WOK*. Brown green onions, and ginger, put in scallops, mushrooms and carrots, saute for 3 minutes. Add sauce and cook until boils. Pour over the broccoli and serve hot.

*refer HOW TO p. 21

SHRIMP PASTE BALLS

INGREDIENTS:

1 ½ lb. shrimp, deveined
¼ C. fresh pork fat, minced
1 Tbsp. green onion, minced
½ tsp. minced ginger
1 cucumber, for garnish
1 can mandarin oranges, for garnish
3 slices of bread

SEASONING:

1 tsp. salt
1 tsp. sugar
¼ tsp. gourmet powder
1 Tbsp. Chinese cooking wine
drops of sesame seed oil
dash pepper
1 ½ Tbsp. Wonder Powder
1 egg white
2 Tbsp. water

METHOD:

1) Use cleaver blade, pound shrimp into a paste. Mix with pork fat, green onion, ginger and all seasoning. Stir and knead well. Shape into balls.
2) Cut bread into very small cubes. Coat balls with these coarse bread crumbs.
3) Heat 4 C. of peanut oil in wok, DEEP FRY* balls at medium/high heat until golden brown. Display on platter garnished with cucumber slices and mandarins. Serve with tobasco sauce or ketchup.

*refer HOW TO p. 21

HOLY MACKEREL

INGREDIENTS:

1 lb. mackerel, cut to ½" slices

MARINATION MIXTURE:

2 green onions, chopped
½ tsp. minced garlic
½ tsp. minced ginger
1 tsp. vinegar
1 Tbsp. Chinese 5 spice powder
1 tsp. sugar

SAUCE:

1 Tbsp. dark soy
1 Tbsp. light soy
2 Tbsp. sugar
½ tsp. salt
dash pepper
¼ tsp. gourmet powder
1 Tbsp. Chinese cooking wine
²/₃ C. water
drops of sesame seed oil
1 Tbsp. ginger juice

METHOD:

1) Marinate fish with marination mixture for ½ hour. Drain and retain marinade for later use.
2) DEEP FRY* fish until golden brown. Drain and set aside.
3) HEAT WOK*, brown green onion, garlic, and ginger. Add sauce and remaining marinade and cook until boil. Return fish and simmer over low heat in wok covered with a lid and cook for 5 mins. Add 1 tsp. vinegar when sauce is nearly dried out. Slightly turn fish and mix well with remaining sauce. Cook until sauce is completely dried up. Serve hot or cold.

*refer HOW TO p. 21

PRAWNS WITH RAINBOW SAUCE

INGREDIENTS:

20 prawns, deveined
¼ C. celery, slivered
¼ C. cucumbers, cored and slivered
¼ C. carrot, slivered
¼ C. onion, slivered
¼ C. green pepper, slivered
¼ C. red pepper, slivered

BATTER:
½ C. YAN's Almighty Powder
   dissolved in ¾ C. water

SAUCE:

½ C. water
1 Tbsp. vinegar
3 Tbsp. sugar
3 Tbsp. tomato ketchup
1 Tbsp. dark soy
2 Tbsp. Wonder Powder

METHOD:

1) Marinate prawns with ½ tsp. salt, dash of pepper and drops sesame seed oil.
2) Coat prawns with batter and DEEP FRY* at medium/high heat until golden brown. Drain and transfer to a platter.
3) HEAT WOK*, saute all vegetables. Add sauce and bring to a boil. Pour over prawns before serving.

*refer HOW TO p. 21

SEAFOOD ON SKEWER

INGREDIENTS:

12 oz. fish filet, cut to 1" cubes
12 oz. fresh prawns, shelled, deveined
1 green pepper, sectioned
½ onion, wedged

SEASONING:

1 Tbsp. green onion, minced
1 tsp. ginger, minced
1 Tbsp. light soy
½ tsp. salt
½ tsp. sugar
dash pepper
drops sesame seed oil
1 tsp. cooking oil

METHOD:

1) Marinate seafood with the above seasoning for ½ hour.
2) Put sea food, green pepper and onion alternatively on skewer.
3) Heat up oil in wok, DEEP FRY* with medium/high heat for 5 minutes. Drain oil and transfer to a platter garnished with pineapple and tomato.

*refer HOW TO p. 21

CURRIED LOBSTER

INGREDIENTS:

2 lb. lobsters, uncooked
3 Tbsp. YAN'S Wonder Powder
1 tsp. salt
1 tsp. minced garlic
1 Tbsp. minced ginger
1 small onion, wedged
1 small green pepper, wedged

SAUCE:

2 Tbsp. curry powder
dash pepper
¼ C cream
1 Tbsp. Chinese cooking wine
1 tsp. sugar
½ tsp. salt
1 Tbsp. Wonder Powder
½ C. water

METHOD:

1) Cut off all the legs with scissors. Cut off the claws and sharp point of head with cleaver. Divide body into 4-5 sections. With the blunt edge of the cleaver, crack the claws.
2) Put lobster in wok lid and dust with YAN'S Wonder Powder and salt.
3) Heat 4 C. peanut oil in wok. DEEP FRY* lobster until color changes. Remove from oil and drain.
4) HEAT WOK*, put in minced ginger, garlic and onion. Add lobster and saute for 1 minute. Add sauce, cover with a lid and cook for a couple of minutes. Add vegetables and sauce, stir mix.

*refer HOW TO p. 21

SCALLOPS WITH PINEAPPLE SAUCE

INGREDIENTS:

1 lb. scallops, cut in half
½ C. pineapple chunks
1 Tbsp. green onion, finely chopped
½ tsp. minced ginger
½ tsp. minced garlic
½ C. toasted flaked almonds

SAUCE:

2 Tbsp. light soy
2 Tbsp. vinegar
½ C. pineapple syrup
2 Tbsp. sugar
1 Tbsp. Wonder Powder

BATTER:
¾ C. YAN's Almighty Powder
   dissolved in ¾ C. water

METHOD:

1) Marinate scallops with 1 tsp. salt, 1 tsp. sugar, ½ tsp. 5 spice powder, 1 Tbsp. Chinese cooking wine and drops of sesame seed oil.
2) Coat scallops with batter and DEEP FRY* at medium/high heat until golden brown. Drain and transfer to platter.
3) HEAT WOK*, put in sauce and cook to a boil, pour over scallops, garnish with flaked almonds.

*refer HOW TO p. 21

SEA FESTIVAL TEPPAN

INGREDIENTS:

½ C. prawns, deveined
½ C. scallops, cut in half
½ C. fish filet, thinly sliced
4 Chinese mushrooms, soaked and
   cut in half
½ carrot, thinly sliced
2 green onions, cut to 2" lengths
1 tsp. minced ginger
1 tsp. minced garlic

SAUCE:

1 tsp. sugar
¼ tsp. gourmet powder
1 ½ Tbsp. Wonder Powder
¼ C. water
1 Tbsp. Chinese cooking wine
dash pepper
1 Tbsp. Oyster Sauce

METHOD:

1) Marinate all seafood with 1 Tbsp. Wonder Powder, ½ tsp. salt and drops
   of sesame seed oil.
2) Heat teppan dish until piping hot.
3) HEAT WOK*, brown green onion, garlic and ginger; put in all ingredients and saute for 2 minutes. Add sauce and bring to a boil. Serve in
   hot teppan dish.

*refer HOW TO p. 21

SHRIMP WITH CASHEW NUTS

INGREDIENTS:

½ lb. raw shrimp, shelled and
   deveined
¼ C. bamboo shoots, diced
½ C. cashew nuts, roasted
2 green onions, cut to 2" lengths
1 tsp. minced ginger
1 tsp. minced garlic
1 egg white

SAUCE:

1 tsp. sugar
¼ tsp. gourmet powder
1 Tbsp. Wonder Powder
dash pepper
drops of sesame seed oil
1 tsp. cooking wine
¼ C. water

METHOD:

1) Marinate shrimp with 1 tsp. Wonder Powder, 1 egg white, ½ tsp. salt, 1
   tsp. Chinese cooking wine and drops of sesame seed oil.
2) HEAT WOK*, brown green onions, garlic and ginger; add shrimps and
   bamboo shoots, saute until shrimps change color.
3) Add sauce and cook until it boils. Stir in cashew nuts.

*refer HOW TO p. 21

SHRIMP WITH MIXED VEGETABLES

INGREDIENTS:

½ lb. shrimp, shelled & deveined
1 tsp. minced ginger
1 tsp. minced garlic
1 green onion, chopped
1 egg white
½ C. carrots, diced
½ C. bamboo shoots, diced
½ C. green peas, frozen

SAUCE:

1 tsp. sugar
¼ tsp. gourmet powder
dash pepper
1 Tbsp. Wonder Powder
1 Tbsp. oyster sauce
¼ C. water

METHOD:

1) Marinate shrimp with 1 Tbsp. Wonder Powder, 1 egg white, ½ tsp. salt, 1 tsp. Chinese cooking wine and drops sesame seed oil.
2) HEAT WOK*, brown green onion, garlic and ginger. Add shrimp and vegetables, saute until shrimp turns red.
3) Add sauce and bring to a boil.

*refer HOW TO p. 21

SALMON WITH BLACK BEAN SAUCE

INGREDIENTS:

2 pieces salmon steak
2 green onions, chopped
2 Tbsp. salted black beans, rinsed and minced
1 Tbsp. minced garlic
1 tsp. minced ginger

SAUCE:

1 tsp. sugar
2 Tbsp. dark soy
1 tsp. Chinese cooking wine
1 Tbsp. YAN'S Wonder Powder
2 Tbsp. water
drops of sesame seed oil

METHOD:

1) Rub salmon with salt.
2) In a bowl, combine black beans, garlic, ginger and half of the green onions. Crush into a paste with handle of cleaver. Mix well with sauce ingredients.
3) Coat salmon with sauce mixture and put on a platter. Steam salmon at high heat for 10-15 minutes.
4) Heat 2 Tbsp. peanut oil and pour over fish before serving.

SESAME SEED HONEY PRAWNS

INGREDIENTS:

12 fresh prawns, shelled
  and deveined
½ C. YAN'S Wonder Powder
²/₃ C. YAN'S Almighty Powder
½ tsp. salt
¼ C. roasted sesame seeds

SAUCE:

1 tsp. sugar
3 Tbsp. honey
1 Tbsp. water
dash salt

SEAFOODS

METHOD:

1) Coat prawns lightly with YAN'S Wonder Powder.
2) Dissolve YAN'S Almighty Powder in equal amount of water to make a smooth batter. Dip prawns in battermix and DEEP FRY* at medium-/high heat until golden brown. Drain and set aside.
3) HEAT WOK*, put in sauce and cook until boil. Return prawns to wok, stir into honey mixture. Remove from wok and sprinkle with roasted sesame seeds.

*refer HOW TO p. 21

SCALLOP DELIGHT

INGREDIENTS:

1 lb. scallops, cut in half
1 Tbsp. ginger, shredded finely
1 tsp. minced garlic
2 green onions, cut to 1" lengths

SAUCE:

1 Tbsp. oyster sauce
1 tsp. sugar
¼ tsp. gourmet powder
drops of sesame seed oil
dash pepper
1 Tbsp. Wonder Powder
1 tsp. Chinese cooking wine
¼ C. water

METHOD:

1) Marinate scallops with 1 Tbsp. Wonder Powder, ½ tsp. salt, 1 tsp. Chinese cooking wine and ½ tsp. sesame seed oil.
2) HEAT WOK*, brown green onion, garlic and ginger; put in scallops and saute for 1 minute. Add sauce and bring to a boil. Serve hot.

*refer HOW TO p. 21

TRICOLOUR PRAWNS

*refer HOW TO p. 21

SEAFOODS

INGREDIENTS:

1 ½ lbs. prawns, shelled
  and deveined
1 ½ C. broccoli, flowerets
2 Tbsp. green onion, chopped
1 tsp. minced ginger
1 tsp. minced garlic
1 egg white
½ tsp. baking soda

SAUCE:

A) ½ tsp. salt
   ½ tsp. sugar
   1 Tbsp. Chinese cooking wine
   drops of sesame seed oil
   1 Tbsp. Wonder Powder
   ¼ C. water
B) 3 Tbsp. tomato ketchup
   2 Tbsps. sugar
C) 1 Tbsp. curry powder

METHOD:

1) Marinate prawns with 2 Tbsp. Wonder Powder, ½ tsp. salt and 1 egg white.
2) Blanch broccoli with boiling water and ½ tsp. baking soda, 1 tsp. salt, 1 tsp. sugar and 1 Tbsp. oil. Drain and display on platter as a divider (dividing the platter into 3 triangular sections).
3) HEAT WOK*, brown green onion, ginger and garlic. Add prawns, saute until they change colour. Add Sauce "A" and bring to a boil. Place ¹/₃ of this mixture in one section of the platter. Remove ¹/₃ of the remaining prawns and set aside. To the prawns remaining in the wok, add Sauce "B" and mix well. Remove from wok and display in another section of the platter.
4) In the same wok, add 1 Tbsp. peanut oil, put in prawns removed earlier. Add Sauce "C". Stir mix. Transfer to remaining section of platter to complete the prawns with 3 different colors.

*refer HOW TO p. 21

CRAB MEAT FOO YUNG

INGREDIENTS:

6 eggs, beaten
½ C. crab meat
¼ C. cooked ham, shredded
1 green onion, chopped fine
½ tsp. minced garlic

SAUCE:

1 tsp. salt
1 tsp. sugar
¼ tsp. gourmet powder
1 Tbsp. oil
sesame seed oil

METHOD:

1) Mix beaten eggs with seasoning.
2) HEAT WOK*, brown garlic and green onion — add crab meat, saute for 2 min. — put in egg and STIR FRY* until set.

*refer HOW TO p. 21

BUTTERED CRAB

INGREDIENTS:

2 lb. crab, whole, uncooked
3 Tbsp. YAN'S Wonder Powder
½ tsp. minced garlic
1 Tbsp. minced ginger
⅓ C. butter, melted
½ tsp. salt
¼ C. water

SAUCE:

1 Tbsp. light soy sauce
1 Tbsp. oyster sauce
dash pepper
1 Tbsp. Chinese cooking wine
1 tsp. sugar
1 Tbsp. Wonder Powder
¼ C. water

METHOD:

1) Prepare crab for cooking*. (refer HOW TO p. 24)
2) With the blunt edge of the cleaver, crack the legs and claws.
3) Sprinkle crab with salt and 2 Tbsp. Wonder Powder
4) Heat 4 C. of oil in hot wok. DEEP FRY* crab for 2 minutes. Remove and drain. Clean wok.
5) HEAT WOK*, add butter, minced garlic, ½ tsp. salt, ¼ C. water and cover with a lid. Cook at high heat for 2 minutes.
6) Add sauce to crab mixture and bring to a boil.

*refer HOW TO p. 21

HOT & SOUR FISH

INGREDIENTS:

1 lb. fish filet, cubed
2 stalks celery, shredded
½ carrot, shredded
1 Sm. onion, shredded

BATTER:
½ C. water
½ C. Almighty Powder

SAUCE:

½ tsp. tobasco sauce
1 Tbsp. light soy
9 Tbsp. sugar
3 Tbsp. tomato paste
1 Tbsp. Wonder Powder
1 Tbsp. vinegar

METHOD:

1) Marinate fish filet with 2 Tbsp. light soy, 4 tsp. 5-spice powder, 1 Tbsp. cooking wine and drops of sesame seed oil.
2) Prepare battermix by dissolving YAN'S Almighty Powder with equal amount of water and stirring until smooth.
3) Heat up oil in wok, coat fish with batter and DEEP FRY* with medium high heat to golden brown. Drain oil and transfer to a platter.
4) HEAT WOK*, put in sauce and cook until boil, pour sauce over deep fried fish and serve.

*refer HOW TO p. 21

PRAWNS WITH BROCCOLI

SEAFOODS

INGREDIENTS:

15 prawns, deveined
1 C. broccoli, flowerets
6 carrot slices
½ C. mushrooms
½ C. baby corn
½ tsp. minced ginger
¼ tsp. minced garlic

SAUCE:

½ tsp. salt
¼ tsp. gourmet powder
1 tsp. sugar
drops of sesame seed oil
1 Tbsp. Wonder Powder
¼ C. water

METHOD:

1) Marinate prawns with ½ tsp. salt, 1 tsp. Wonder Powder.
2) HEAT WOK*, brown ginger, garlic, put in prawns, saute for 2 minutes at light heat and sprinkle with 1 Tbsp. Chinese cooking wine. Remove and set aside.
3) HEAT WOK*, STIR FRY* vegetables, return prawns to wok, add sauce and bring to a boil.

*refer HOW TO p. 21

PRAWNS WITH MUSHROOMS

INGREDIENTS:

15 prawns, deveined
1 C. mushrooms
4 oz. Chinese mushrooms, soaked for 2 hours
8 pieces broccoli, flowerets
½ tsp. salt
½ tsp. minced ginger

SAUCE:

1 Tbsp. Wonder Powder
1 Tbsp. oyster sauce
½ tsp. sugar
1 Tbsp. Chinese cooking wine
¼ C. water

METHOD:

1) Marinate prawns with 1 Tbsp. Wonder Powder, ½ tsp. salt, and 1 Tbsp. Chinese cooking wine.
2) Blanch broccoli in boiling water with ¼ tsp. baking soda, ½ tsp. salt and 2 Tbsp. oil; drain and display on platter.
3) HEAT WOK*, brown ginger, put in mushrooms and prawns, saute for 3 minutes. Add sauce and cook until boils. Pour over the broccoli and serve hot.

*refer HOW TO p. 21

BUTTERFLY PRAWNS

INGREDIENTS:

10-15 prawns, fresh uncooked
10-15 slices of white bread
10-15 ham slices
2 eggs, medium
1 Tbsp. Wonder Powder

METHOD:

1) Remove shells of all the prawns, but carefully retain the tail part.
2) Put the abdominal side down on a board. Use a sharp knife to slit the back part all the way down to the abdominal part, cutting it almost into half. Remove the black vein and put it aside for later use.
3) Dissolve Wonder Powder into the eggs and beat thoroughly.
4) Toast the bread and put aside for later use.
5) When ready to do cooking, fill the wok with 2" of oil and heat up the oil with medium/high heat until smoke begins to rise.
6) Carefully dip prawns, one at a time, into the egg mixture and then place it on top of bread with the OPEN side down. Then dip a piece of ham into the egg mixture and place it on top of the prawn. Place the whole combination gently into the hot oil with the prawn side down first and deep fry until the edges of bread turn brown. Turn over and fry for 5 seconds. Serve hot.

SEAFOOD IN A NEST

INGREDIENTS:

4 oz. scallops, fresh, cut in half
6 prawns, fresh, deveined
6 slices fish filet, thinly sliced
6 baby corn
4 broccoli flowerets
¼ C. mushrooms, fresh
3 green onions, cut to 2" lengths
½ tsp. minced ginger
½ tsp. minced garlic
½ egg white

SAUCE:

½ tsp. salt
½ tsp. sugar
¼ tsp. gourmet powder
1 Tbsp. Chinese cooking wine
drops of sesame seed oil
1 Tbsp. starch solution

METHOD:

1) Prepare POTATO BASKET* (refer HOW TO p. 22)
2) Marinate all seafood with 1 tsp. Wonder Powder, ½ tsp. salt, ½ egg white and drops of sesame seed oil.
3) HEAT WOK*, brown green onion, garlic and ginger, put in seafood and saute until changes colour. Remove and set aside.
4) With same wok, add 1 Tbsp. peanut oil. STIR FRY* vegetables; return seafood to wok. Add sauce and bring to a boil, transfer to basket and serve hot.

*refer HOW TO p. 21

SEAFOODS

LETTUCE WRAP WITH VEGETABLES

INGREDIENTS:

½ C. mushrooms, minced
8 Chinese mushrooms, soaked
  and minced
½ C. celery, chopped fine
½ C. water chestnuts,
  chopped fine
½ C. carrots, chopped fine
½ C. roasted walnuts,
  chopped fine
½ head of lettuce
1 green onion, cut to 1" lengths
1 tsp. minced ginger

SAUCE:

½ tsp. salt
1 Tbsp. dark soy sauce
2 Tbsp. hoi sin sauce
½ tsp. 5 spice powder
½ tsp. sesame seed oil
1 Tbsp. Chinese cooking wine
¼ C. water
1 tsp. Wonder Powder

VEGETABLES

METHOD:

1) Peel leaves from lettuce individually and soak in cold water until ready to serve.
2) HEAT WOK*, brown green onion and ginger for a few seconds. STIR FRY* vegetables.
3) Add sauce and bring to boil, then add walnuts and mix well.
4) Put 1-2 Tbsp. of mixture on each lettuce leaf, wrap and serve immediately.

*refer HOW TO p. 21

SWEET AND SOUR VEGETABLES

INGREDIENTS:

1 cauliflower, flowerets
1 cucumber, sliced
1 carrot, sliced
½ C. bamboo shoots, sliced
½ C. water chestnuts, sliced
1 green onion, cut to 1" lengths
½ tsp. minced ginger

SAUCE:

3 Tbsp. brown sugar
1 Tbsp. vinegar
½ tsp. salt
1 ½ Tbsp. Wonder Powder
½ C. water

METHOD:

1) HEAT WOK*, brown green onion and ginger for few seconds.
2) STIR FRY* vegetables.
3) Add sauce and bring to a boil.

*refer HOW TO p. 21

FOUR TREASURES FOR VEGETARIANS

INGREDIENTS:

¾ C. broccoli, flowerets
¾ C. cauliflower, flowerets
¾ C. fresh mushrooms
¾ C. baby corn
1 green onion, cut to 1" lengths
1 tsp. minced ginger
½ tsp. minced garlic
½ tsp. baking soda

SAUCE:

1 tsp. light soy
2 Tbsp. oyster sauce
1½ tsp. sugar
⅔ C. water
½ tsp. sesame seed oil
1 tsp. Chinese cooking wine
2 Tbsp. Wonder Powder

METHOD:

1) Boil 2 C. of water in a wok, add ½ tsp. baking soda, 1 tsp. salt and 2 Tbsp. oil. Blanch all vegetables for 2 minutes. Drain and separate vegetables into 4 sections on a platter.

2) HEAT WOK*, brown green onion and ginger for a few seconds. Add sauce and bring to boil. Pour sauce over vegetables and serve hot.

VEGETABLE CREPES

INGREDIENTS:

2 eggs, beaten
1 C. cabbage, shredded
½ C. onion, shredded
1 C. celery, slivered
2 C. bean sprouts
1 green onion, cut to 1"
   lengths
½ tsp. minced ginger
16 sheets egg roll skin,
   steamed until softened
   (refer HOW TO p. 22)

SAUCE:

1 Tbsp. dark soy sauce
2 Tbsp. hoi sin sauce
1 Tbsp. oyster sauce
1 Tbsp. Chinese cooking wine
½ tsp. sesame seed oil
¼ C. water
1 Tbsp. Wonder Powder
½ tsp. salt

METHOD:

1) Smear 1 tsp. of peanut oil on the surface of the wok. Use medium heat to cook egg as to form an egg sheet. Remove and cut into strips.

2) HEAT WOK*, brown onions and ginger. Add all vegetables and STIR FRY*.

3) When cooked, add egg strips and mix well.

4) Place 1-2 Tbsp. of mixture on wrapper. Wrap and serve hot as a crepe.

*refer HOW TO p. 21

VEGETABLES

BUDDHIST TEMPLE

INGREDIENTS:

20 Chinese mushrooms, soaked
    in hot water for 1-2 hrs.,
    drained
2 C. broccoli flowerets
1 C. baby corn
1 C. fresh mushrooms
2 green onions, cut into
    2" lengths
1 tsp. minced ginger

SEASONING:

1 tsp. light soy sauce
2 Tbsp. oyster sauce
1½ tsp. sugar
1 Tbsp. dark soy sauce
1 tsp. Chinese cooking wine
½ tsp. sesame seed oil
½ C. water
1½ Tbsp. Wonder Powder

METHOD:

1) Boil 2 C. of water in a wok, add 1 tsp. salt and 2 Tbsp. oil. Blanch all vegetables for 2 minutes. Drain and display broccoli around edge of platter to form circle.

2) HEAT WOK*, brown green onions and ginger for a few seconds. Add all mushrooms to the wok and STIR FRY*. Add sauce mixture, stir and bring to boil.

3) Arrange Chinese mushrooms on top, and slightly inside broccoli circle with tops facing up. Continuing a pyramid formation place baby corn on top, and slightly inside circle of Chinese mushrooms. Place fresh mushrooms at very top and pour sauce over vegetable temple before serving.

*refer HOW TO p. 21

BUDDHIST FEAST

INGREDIENTS:

1 C. broccoli, flowerets
½ C. bamboo shoots, sliced
½ C. water chestnuts, sliced
1 carrot, sliced diagonally
6 Chinese mushrooms, soaked
    and sliced
½ C. fresh mushrooms
½ C. baby corn
1 stalk green onion, cut to 1" lengths
½ tsp. minced ginger
10 Lily Buds, soaked
6 Cloud Ears, soaked
½ C. cellophane noodles, soaked

SAUCE:

1½ tsp. sugar
2 Tbsp. oyster sauce
1 Tbsp. dark soy sauce
1 tsp. Chinese cooking wine
½ tsp. sesame seed oil
¼ C. water
1 Tbsp. Wonder Powder

METHOD:

1) HEAT WOK*, brown green onion and ginger for few seconds. Put in all vegetables and STIR FRY*.

2) When done, add sauce and bring to a boil. Serve hot.

*refer HOW TO p. 21

GREEN CORAL

INGREDIENTS:

2 C. broccoli flowerets
½ C. crab meat
1 egg white, beaten
½ tsp. garlic, minced
½ tsp. ginger, minced
1 green onion, cut to 1"
¼ tsp. baking soda

SAUCE:

½ tsp. salt
½ tsp. sugar
¼ tsp. gourmet powder
1 tsp. Chinese cooking wine
drops of sesame seed oil
dash pepper
½ C. water
1 ½ tsp. Wonder Powder

METHOD:

1) Blanch broccoli in 4 C. water with ¼ tsp. baking soda, 1 tsp. salt and 2 Tbsp. oil for 5 min. Drain and arrange in circular pattern on a platter.
2) HEAT WOK*, brown green onion, garlic and ginger; put in crab meat and saute for 1 minute. Add sauce and bring to a boil. Stir in egg white. Pour sauce on top of broccoli to serve.

*refer HOW TO p. 21

VEGETABLES

WALNUT VEGETABLE CHOP SUEY

INGREDIENTS:

½ C. walnuts, shelled, blanched
  and skinned
½ C. water chestnuts, sliced
4 Chinese mushrooms, soaked,
  cut in half
1 carrot, sliced, blanched
1 green pepper, sectioned
1 green onion, cut to 1"
¼ tsp. garlic, minced
¼ tsp. ginger, minced

SAUCE:

¼ tsp. salt
½ tsp. sugar
1 tsp. light soy
2 tsp. oyster sauce
1 tsp. Chinese cooking wine
drops of sesame seed oil
1 tsp. Wonder Powder
¼ C. water

METHOD:

1) Heat oil on medium/high heat and DEEP FRY* walnuts until brown. Drain and set aside.
2) With same wok, add 2 Tbsp. peanut oil. STIR FRY* vegetables. Add sauce and bring to a boil. Return walnuts to wok. Mix well. Serve.

*refer HOW TO p. 21

MUSHROOMS IN A NEST

INGREDIENTS:

1 C. straw mushrooms, diced
½ C. fresh mushrooms, diced
4 oz. Chinese mushrooms,
   soaked 2 hrs., diced
½ C. broccoli, flowerets
¾ C. carrots, diced
½ C. cashew nuts or walnuts
1 green onion, cut to 1" lengths
½ tsp. minced garlic
½ tsp. minced ginger
*potatoes for making basket

SAUCE:

1 tsp. light soy sauce
1 tsp. dark soy sauce
1 Tbsp. oyster sauce
1 tsp. Chinese cooking wine
drops sesame seed oil
1 Tbsp. Wonder Powder
¼ C. water
½ tsp. sugar

METHOD:

1) Prepare basket*.(refer HOW TO p. 22)
2) HEAT WOK*, brown green onion, garlic and ginger. Stir in all ingredients, except nuts. STIR FRY*. When cooked, add sauce and bring to a boil. Add nuts and mix well.
3) Transfer to basket to serve.

* refer HOW TO p. 21

WEST LAKE BEEF SOUP

INGREDIENTS:

²/₃ C. ground beef
1 green onion, minced
2 egg whites, beaten

SEASONING:

1 cube chicken bouillon
1 tsp. salt
1 tsp. sugar
dash pepper
¼ tsp. gourmet powder

METHOD:

1) Marinate beef with 1 Tbsp. Wonder Powder, 1 Tbsp. light soy sauce, and 1 Tbsp. Chinese cooking wine.
2) Bring 5 C. water to boil in wok and stir in ground beef, loosen beef with spatula. Add seasoning and boil for 5 minutes.
3) Thicken soup with 2 Tbsp. Wonder Powder diluted in ¹/₃ C. water. Stir in egg whites. Sprinkle with green onion.

VEGETABLES

COLOURFUL SHRIMP SOUP

INGREDIENTS:

½ C. fresh shrimp meat
¼ C. bamboo shoots, diced
¼ C. carrot, diced
¼ C. frozen peas
1 egg white, beaten
10 Won Ton wrappers, cut into
   1½" squares and deep fried
   until golden brown
2 Tbsp. Wonder Powder

SEASONING:

1 tsp. sugar
1 cube chicken bouillon
1 tsp. salt
drops of sesame seed oil
dash pepper
¼ tsp. gourmet powder

THICKENING:

2 Tbsp. Wonder Powder
⅓ C. water

METHOD:

1) Bring 4 C. water to boil in wok. Add all vegetables, seasoning and shrimp. Cook for 5 minutes.
2) Thicken soup with Wonder Powder, stir in egg whites. Garnish with won tons and serve hot.

BEAN CURD SOUP

INGREDIENTS:

1 C. bean curd, cut 1" cubes
1 carrot, blanched and sliced
½ C. fresh mushrooms, cut in half
¼ C. bok choy or broccoli, cut
   2" slices
½ tsp. minced ginger
1 Tbsp. green onion, chopped

SEASONING:

1 tsp. salt
1 tsp. sugar
1 cube chicken bouillon
¼ tsp. gourmet powder
drops of sesame seed oil

METHOD:

1) Bring 4 C. water to boil in wok. Add all seasoning except sesame seed oil.
2) Add ginger and all vegetables (except bean curd and green onion). Boil for 1 minute.
3) Add bean curd and cook for half minute. Sprinkle with drops of sesame seed oil and green onion. Serve.

SOUP

SIZZLING RICE SOUP

INGREDIENTS:

8 pcs. 2" square Rice Cake*
  (refer HOW TO p. 22)
¼ C. chicken, sliced
¼ C. cooked ham, sliced
¼ C. pork, sliced
¼ C. shrimp, fresh
¼ C. bamboo shoots, sliced
4 Chinese mushrooms, soaked
  and cut in half

SEASONING:

1 cube chicken bouillon
½ tsp. salt
½ tsp. sugar
1 Tbsp. dark soy sauce
drops sesame seed oil
dash pepper

METHOD:

1) Marinate pork and chicken with 1 Tbsp. Wonder Powder, 1 Tbsp. light soy sauce and 1 Tbsp. Chinese cooking wine for 15 minutes.
2) Bring 2 Cups of water of boil in wok. Add meat, ingredients and seasoning and boil for 5 minutes.
3) Thicken soup with 2 Tbsp. Wonder Powder diluted in ⅓ C. water and transfer to casserole.
4) HEAT WOK* with 2 C. oil at high heat. DEEP FRY* rice cake until golden brown. Rain and put in warm casserole.
5) When ready to serve, pour soup over the rice cake.

*refer HOW TO p. 21

*refer HOW TO p. 21

SOUP

LETTUCE MEAT BALL SOUP

INGREDIENTS:

1 C. ground pork
½ head of lettuce
  (leaves separate)
¼ C. water chestnuts
6 Chinese mushrooms,
  soaked and chopped
1 egg, beaten

SEASONING:

½ tsp. salt
1 cube chicken bouillon
¼ tsp. gourmet powder
drops sesame seed oil

METHOD:

1) Mix pork, with 1 Tbsp. of Wonder Powder, 2 Tbsp. light soy sauce, 1 egg, water chestnuts and Chinese mushrooms. Knead well and form into small meat balls.
2) Bring 5 C. water to a boil in wok. Add meat balls and seasoning. Cook for 5 minutes, then add lettuce leaves.

SEAFOOD SOUP

INGREDIENTS:

6 prawns, deveined
6 scallops, cut in half
6 slices fish filet
½ tsp. ginger, slivers
1 C. bok choy or broccoli
   (cut in 2" lengths)
1 tsp. green onion, chopped

SEASONING:

1 tsp. Chinese cooking wine
½ tsp. salt
1 tsp. sugar
1 cube chicken bouillon
¼ tsp. gourmet powder
drops of sesame seed oil

METHOD:

1) Marinate seafood with ½ tsp. salt, ½ tsp. sugar, 1 Tbsp. Chinese cooking wine and 1 Tbsp. Wonder Powder for 15 minutes.

2) Bring 5 C. water to boil. Add all ingredients and seasoning, boil for 3 minutes.

WINTER MELON SOUP

INGREDIENTS:

1 C. winter melon
   (available in Chinatown)
or 1 C. cucumber, peeled, cored
and diced (as substitute)
¼ C. frozen peas
¼ C. carrots, blanched & diced
½ C. lean pork, diced
¼ C. shrimp meat, diced
4 Chinese mushrooms, soaked
   and diced
4 slivers of ginger
1 tsp. green onions, chopped

SEASONING:

½ tsp. salt
1 tsp. sugar
1 cube chicken bouillon
¼ tsp. gourmet powder
drops of sesame seed oil

METHOD:

1) Marinate pork with 1 tsp. Wonder Powder, 1 tsp. light soy sauce and 1 tsp. Chinese cooking wine for 15 minutes.

2) Bring 5 C. water to boil in wok. Put in pork and seasoning. Cook for 5 minutes. Add all vegetables and shrimp. Cook another 2 minutes.

soup

MEAT BALL SOUP

INGREDIENTS:

4 oz. minced pork
2 oz. cooked ham, minced
1 oz. water chestnut, minced
1 C. spinach
8 slices carrot
2 slices ginger

SEASONING:

1 cube chicken bouillon
½ tsp. salt
½ tsp. sugar
drops of sesame seed oil
dash pepper

METHOD:

1) Mix minced pork, ham and water chestnut with 2 tsp. light soy, ½ tsp. sugar, ¼ tsp. gourmet powder, 1 Tbsp. YAN'S Wonder Powder and drops of sesame seed oil. Stir until meat condensed — form into small balls.
2) Bring 4 C. water to a boil, put in meat balls and cook until they float.
3) Add all seasoning, spinach and carrot. Bring to boil.

SNAKE MEAT SOUP

INGREDIENTS:

1 Pack Dry Snake (available in Chinatown)
10 won ton wrappers
1 Tbsp. green onion, chopped

SEASONING:

1 cube chicken bouillon
1 tsp. cooking wine
1 Tbsp. dark soy
drops of sesame seed oil
2 Tbsp. Wonder Powder
1/3 C. water

METHOD:

1) Cook dry snake with 3 C. water and 2 Tbsp. cooking oil for 15 minutes. Add seasoning and chicken soup with Wonder Powder.
2) Heat up 2 C. oil. Cut won ton wrappers in ½" squares. DEEP FRY* with light heat until golden brown.
3) Sprinkle deep fried won ton wrappers and green onions on soup. Serve.

*refer HOW TO p. 21

CRAB MEAT AND CORN SOUP

INGREDIENTS:

4 oz. crab meat
1 can creamed corn
4 C. chicken broth
2 Tbsp. green onion, chopped
1 egg white

SEASONING:

dash pepper
drops of sesame seed oil
1 tsp. salt
dash gourmet powder
2 Tbsp. Wonder Powder
¼ C. water

METHOD:

1) In a wok and bring chicken broth to a boil. Add creamed corn and crab meat. Bring to a boil again.
2) Add seasoning and cook until soup is thickened. Stir in egg white. Sprinkle with green onions before serving.

*refer HOW TO p. 21

BEEF WITH WATERCRESS SOUP

INGREDIENTS:

4 oz. beef, sliced
2 C. watercress
½ tsp. ginger, slivered

SEASONING:

1 cube chicken bouillon
1 tsp. salt
1 tsp. sugar
¼ tsp. gourmet powder
few drops of sesame seed oil

METHOD:

1) Marinate beef with 1 tsp. Wonder Powder, 1 Tbsp. light soy sauce and 1 Tbsp. Chinese cooking wine for 15 minutes.
2) Bring 4 C. water to a boil in wok. Add beef, ginger and all seasoning. Boil for 5 minutes. Serve.

HAM & BEAN CURD SOUP

INGREDIENTS:

1 bean curd, cut to 2" slices
½ C. ham, sliced to 1"
1 C. Chinese cabbage, cut to 2"
2 slices ginger

SEASONING:

1 C. chicken broth
½ tsp. salt
½ tsp. sugar
1 tsp. cooking wine
drops of sesame seed oil
dash pepper

METHOD:

1) Bring 4 C. water to a boil, add seasoning and Chinese cabbage and cook until boil.
2) Add bean curd and ham and cook for ½ minute.

MOON ON MIRROR SOUP

INGREDIENTS:

4 Quail eggs or peewee eggs
8 slices carrot
1 C. spinach
½ C. straw mushrooms

SEASONING:

1 cube chicken bouillon
1 tsp. salt
1 tsp. sugar
¼ tsp. gourmet powder
drops of sesame seed oil
dash pepper

METHOD:

1) Crack quail eggs on oiled small dishes. Steam in wok for 10 minutes, until set. Remove from dishes and set aside.

2) Bring 4 C. of water to a boil in wok. Add seasoning, spinach, carrot and straw mushrooms and cook for 5 minutes.

3) Add eggs and serve.

HOT & SOUR SOUP

INGREDIENTS:

4 oz. lean pork, shredded
¼ C. tofu (bean curd), shredded
1 egg, beaten
4 Chinese dried mushrooms,
   soaked and shredded
2 Tbsp. carrot, shredded
2 green onions, chopped
2 Tbsp. ham, cooked and shredded
2 Tbsp. bamboo shoots, shredded

SEASONING:

1 Tbsp. dark soy
1 cube chicken bouillon
¾ tsp. salt
¼ tsp. gourmet powder
1 tsp. sugar
3 Tbsp. vinegar
dash pepper
drops sesame seed oil
drops chili sauce OR tobasco
3 Tbsp. Wonder Powder
diluted in 1/3 C. water

METHOD:

1) Marinate shredded pork with 1 tsp. Wonder Powder, and 1 Tbsp. light soy sauce for 15 minutes.

2) Bring 4 C. water to boil in wok. Add all ingredients (except bean curd, green onion and egg) and cook for 5 minutes.

3) Add seasoning and bean curd. Thicken soup with Wonder Powder, stir in beaten egg. Sprinkle with green onions and serve.

BANANA CHICKEN (page 86)

FOUR TREASURES FOR VEGETARIANS (page 51)

TRICOLOUR PRAWNS (page 46)

CURRIED BEEF TRIANGLES (page 109)

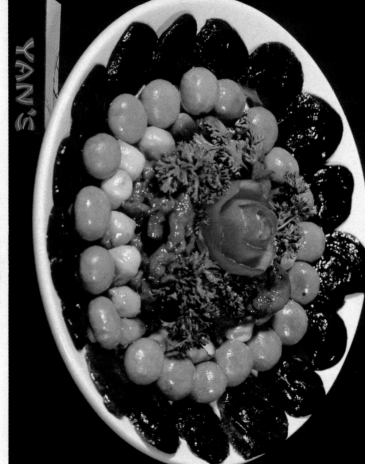

BEEF WITH MUSHROOMS (page 95)

PRAWNS BOUQUET (page 30)

YAN's

SHRIMP PASTE BALLS (page 40)

BUDDHIST TEMPLE (page 52)

TOMATO EGG DROP SOUP

INGREDIENTS:

2 tomatoes, cut to 6 wedges
2 medium eggs, beaten with
    dash of salt
1 green onion, chopped fine
½ C. green peas

SEASONING:

1 cube chicken bouillon
1 tsp. salt
1 Tbsp. sugar
1 Tbsp. vinegar
¼ tsp. gourmet powder
1 tsp. cooking wine
drops of sesame seed oil
dash pepper

METHOD:

1) In a wok, bring 4 C. water to a boil, put in seasoning and tomato. Cook for 1 minute.

2) Slowly pour the beaten eggs in a thin stream. Stir slowly in a circular motion until the eggs congeal into thin ribbons.

3) Garnish with green onion and serve.

TOMATO MEAT BALL SOUP

INGREDIENTS:

½ C. hamburger meat
¼ C. water chestnuts, minced
2 tomatoes, cut to 6 wedges
1 stalk green onion,
    chopped fine

SEASONING:

1 cube chicken bouillon
1 tsp. salt
1 Tbsp. sugar
1 Tbsp. vinegar
¼ tsp. gourmet powder
1 tsp. cooking wine
drops of sesame seed oil
dash pepper

METHOD:

1) Marinate hamburger meat with 1 Tbsp. Wonder Powder, 1 Tbsp. light soy, 1 tsp. cooking wine and drops of sesame seed oil.

2) Mix hamburger meat with minced water chestnut. Knead well to condense meat. Form small meat balls.

3) In wok, bring 4 C. water to boil, put in meat balls and cook until it floats top of soup. Add tomato and cook for 1 minute.

4) Add seasoning and garnish with chopped green onion. Serve.

SHREDDED CHICKEN SOUP

INGREDIENTS:

4 oz. chicken meat, shredded
4 Chinese mushrooms, soaked
   and shredded
¼ C. bamboo shoots, shredded
1 Tbsp. green onion, chopped
¼ tsp. ginger slivers
2 Tbsp. Wonder Powder

SEASONING:

1 cube chicken bouillon
1 tsp. salt
1 tsp. sugar
1 Tbsp. dark soy
drops sesame seed oil
dash pepper
¼ tsp. gourmet powder

METHOD:

1) Marinate chicken with 1 tsp. Wonder Powder, 1 Tbsp. light soy sauce and 1 tsp. Chinese cooking wine for 15 minutes.

2) Bring 5 C. water to boil, in wok. Add all ingredients (except Wonder Powder) and seasoning. Cook for 5 minutes.

3) Thicken soup with 2 Tbsp. Wonder Powder diluted in ⅓ C. water.

PORK STUFFED CUCUMBERS

INGREDIENTS:

2 cucumbers, peeled
10 oz. ground pork
2 Chinese mushrooms, soaked
and minced
1 Tbsp. green onion,
finely chopped
½ tsp. minced ginger
¾ C. frozen mixed peas, carrots
& corn.

SEASONING:

1 tsp. salt
1 tsp. sugar
1 Tbsp. Wonder Powder
1 Tbsp. Chinese cooking wine
drops of sesame seed oil
dash pepper
1 egg, beaten

SAUCE:

½ tsp. sugar
1 Tbsp. light soy
1 tsp. Chinese cooking wine
drops sesame·seed oil
½ C. water
1½ Tbsp. Wonder Powder
½ tsp. salt
1 Tbsp. oyster sauce

METHOD:

1) Mix well, pork with Chinese mushrooms, green onions, ginger and seasoning. Stir well to a firm filling.

2) Cut cucumber in 1" sections, scoop out seeds. Dust hole with YAN'S Wonder Powder, fill with filling mixture.

3) Arrange on a platter and steam for 20-25 minutes over high heat. Reserve juice on platter for making sauce.

4) HEAT WOK*, stir in mixed peas, carrots and corn. Add sauce and juice (from steaming), bring to a boil. Pour over stuffed cucumbers.

*refer HOW TO p. 21

PORK

PORK CUBES WITH PLUM SAUCE

INGREDIENTS:

1 lb. pork tenderloin,
cubed 1" size
½ tsp. minced garlic
2 Tbsp. YAN'S Wonder Powder

SEASONING:

1 Tbsp. Chinese cooking wine
2 Tbsp. light soy sauce
1 Tbsp. dark soy sauce
2 Tbsp. hoi sin sauce
¼ tsp. salt
½ C. plum sauce
1 Tbsp. Wonder Powder
¼ C. water

METHOD:

1) Marinate pork with YAN'S Wonder Powder, Chinese cooking wine, light soy sauce, dark soy sauce, hoi sin sauce, sugar, salt and drops of sesame seed oil for 1 hour.

2) HEAT WOK*, add minced garlic and pork. STIR FRY* for 10 minutes.

3) Add sauce to pork and bring to boil. Serve on a Teppan, if available.

*refer HOW TO p. 21

63

SATAY PORK ON SKEWER

INGREDIENTS:

1 lb. pork tenderloin, cut
   to 1" x ½" thick slices
12 bamboo skewers
2 Tbsp. satay powder OR sauce
½ cucumber, sliced for garnish

SAUCE:

3 Tbsp. satay sauce
¼ tsp. salt
1 Tbsp. sugar
½ C. water
drop of yellow food coloring
1 ½ Tbsp. Wonder Powder

METHOD:

1) Marinate pork with 3 Tbsp. light soy, 2 Tbsp. satay powder, 1 Tbsp. Chinese cooking wine and ½ tsp. sesame seed oil.
2) Arrange pork on skewer.
3) Heat 3 C. of peanut oil and DEEP FRY* pork at medium/high heat until golden brown. Drain and transfer to a platter garnished with cucumber slices.
4) HEAT WOK*, add sauce from pork marination and bring to a boil. Pour over pork skewers.

*refer HOW TO p. 21

STUFFED SPARERIBS

INGREDIENTS:

2 lbs. spareribs cut to 2"
½ C. Bamboo shoots, cut to
   2" strips
5 stalks green onion, cut to
   2" strips
1 C. YAN'S Almighty Powder

SEASONING:

1 tsp. salt
1 tsp. sugar
1 Tbsp. dark soy
1 Tbsp. Chinese cooking wine
drops of sesame seed oil

METHOD:

1) Bring 4 C. water to boil in wok, add seasoning and cook spareribs until bone can be removed. Approximately 15 minutes.
2) Remove bone from spareribs and insert bamboo shoot and green onion into the hole.
3) Prepare battermix by dissolving YAN'S Almighty Powder with equal amount of water and stirring until smooth.
4) Heat up oil in wok, coat stuffed spareribs with batter and DEEP FRY* with medium/high heat to golden brown. Drain. Serve with worchestershire sauce.

*refer HOW TO p. 21

THREE IS COMPANY

INGREDIENTS:

4 oz. cooked ham, cut to
    1 x 2½" slices
2 oz. Chinese mushrooms, soaked
    and cut in half
1 C. bamboo shoots, cut to
    1 x 2½" slices, blanched
2 C. broccoli, flowerets, blanched
1 green onion, cut to 1" lengths
½ tsp. minced ginger

SAUCE:

2 Tbsp. light soy
1 tsp. sugar
2 Tbsp. oyster sauce
1 tsp. Chinese cooking wine
drops sesame seed oil
½ C. water
1½ Tbsp. Wonder Powder

METHOD:

1) Cook Chinese mushrooms with ½ C. water, ½ tsp. light soy, ¼ tsp. gourmet powder, 1 tsp. cooking wine and drops of sesame seed oil for 15 minutes. Drain and cool.
2) Sandwich ham, bamboo shoots and mushrooms, arrange in two rows on an oval platter and garnish with broccoli flowerets.
3) Steam over high heat for 10 minutes, drain juice and reserve.
4) HEAT WOK*, with 1 Tbsp. of peanut oil, brown green onions and ginger; add sauce and juice, bring to a boil. Pour over sandwich before serving.

*refer HOW TO p. 21

PORK

STEAMED GARLIC SPARERIBS

INGREDIENTS:

1 lb. spareribs, chopped 1¼ sq.
½ tsp. Chinese cooking wine
¼ tsp. gourmet powder
1 Tbsp. salted black beans,
    rinsed and minced
½ tsp. minced garlic
½ tsp. minced ginger
1 tsp. sugar
1 tsp. green onion, chopped fine

2 Tbsp. light soy sauce
1 Tbsp. dark soy sauce
1 Tbsp. Wonder Powder
1 Tbsp. vegetable oil
2 Tbsp. water

METHOD:

1) Marinate spareribs with all ingredients (except green onion) for half hour.
2) Put all ingredients on plate and steam over wok at high heat for 15 minutes. Sprinkle the green onion over the spareribs before serving.

CHILI PORK

INGREDIENTS:

12 oz. pork tenderloin, diced
4 dried chili peppers
¼ C. bamboo shoots, diced
¼ C. carrots, blanched & diced
2 green onions, cut to 1" lengths
½ tsp. minced garlic
½ tsp. minced ginger
½ C. roasted peanuts, unsalted

SAUCE:

1½ Tbsp. dark soy
¼ tsp. gourmet powder
1 Tbsp. sugar
1 tsp. Chinese cooking wine
drops of sesame seed oil
1 tsp. tobasco sauce
¼ C. water
1 Tbsp. Wonder Powder

METHOD:

1) Marinate diced pork with 1 tsp. Wonder Powder, 2 Tbsp. light soy, 1 Tbsp. cooking wine and drops of sesame seed oil.
2) STIR FRY*, chili peppers until dark, then put in green onion, garlic and ginger; saute for a few seconds. Add pork and saute until meat changes color.
3) Add all vegetables, mix well with pork and STIR FRY*.
4) When done, add sauce and bring to a boil. Garnish with roasted peanuts and serve hot.

*refer HOW TO p. 21

FRUITED PORK

INGREDIENTS:

1 lb. pork, tenderloin, cut
  to 1½" cubes
¹/₃ C. canned apricots,
  cut to 1" cubes
¹/₃ C. pineapple chunks
¹/₃ C. frozen snow peas,
  thawed, cut in half
1 clove garlic, minced

SAUCE:

2 tsp. light soy sauce
½ C. apricot syrup
1 Tbsp. lemon juice
1 tsp. Wonder powder
½ tsp. sugar

METHOD:

1) Marinate pork cubes with 1 tsp. Wonder Powder, 2 Tbsp. light soy 1 Tbsp. Chinese cooking wine and drops of sesame seed oil.
2) HEAT WOK*, brown garlic, put in pork and saute until meat changes color. Add 3 Tbsp. water, cover with a lid and cook until steam comes out from the edge of the lid. Then add snow peas and saute for ½ minute. Add sauce and bring to a boil.
3) Add apricots and pineapple. Mix well with pork and snow peas.

*refer HOW TO p. 21

IMPERIAL SPARE RIBS

INGREDIENTS:

1½-2 lb. spare ribs, cut to
 sections 3-4" in length
3 Tbsp. light soy sauce
1 Tbsp. dark soy sauce
1 Tbsp. Chinese cooking wine
1 tsp. minced garlic
½ tsp. Chinese 5 spice powder
1 egg, beaten
3 Tbsp. YAN'S Wonder Powder

SAUCE:

4 Tbsp. sugar
1 Tbsp. worchestershire sauce
2 Tbsp. tomato paste
drops sesame seed oil
1 Tbsp. vinegar
½ tsp. salt
½ C. water
1 Tbsp. Wonder Powder

METHOD:

1) Marinate spare ribs with light soy, dark soy, salt, sesame seed oil, egg, sugar, cooking wine, 5 spice powder, and garlic. Marinate for 1 hour.
2) Coat spare ribs lightly with YAN'S Wonder Powder. Deep fry in 4 C. of hot peanut oil at medium heat for 5 minutes. Then DEEP FRY* at high heat for an additional 2 minutes. Remove and drain on paper towel.
3) Clean and HEAT WOK*, bring sauce ingredients to a boil. Return spare ribs, stir mix well and serve hot.

*refer HOW TO p. 21

PORK WITH BROCCOLI

PORK

INGREDIENTS:

6 oz. pork butt, sliced
1½ C. broccoli, flowerets
½ carrot, sliced
1 green onion, cut to 1" lengths
½ C. onion, wedged
½ tsp. minced garlic
½ tsp. minced ginger

SAUCE:

½ tsp. salt
1 Tbsp. oyster sauce
¼ tsp. gourmet powder
1 tsp. Chinese cooking wine
drops sesame seed oil
1 Tbsp. Wonder Powder
¼ C. water
1 tsp. sugar

METHOD:

1) Marinate pork with 1 tsp. Wonder Powder, 1 Tbsp. light soy, 1 tsp. cooking wine and drops sesame seed oil.
2) HEAT WOK*, brown green onion, garlic and ginger; put in pork and saute until meat changes color. Add vegetables and STIR FRY*.
3) When done, add sauce and bring to a boil. Serve hot.

*refer HOW TO p. 21

PORK WITH BAMBOO SHOOTS

INGREDIENTS:

1 lb. pork shoulder,
  cut to 1½" cubes
1 C. bamboo shoots, cut to
  1" cubes
2 green onions, cut to 1" lengths
1 tsp. minced garlic
1 tsp. minced ginger

SAUCE:

2 Tbsp. dark soy
½ Tbsp. sugar
½ tsp. salt
drops of sesame seed oil
1 Tbsp. Wonder Powder
1 tsp. Chinese cooking wine
¼ C. water
2 Tbsp. oyster sauce

METHOD:

1) Marinate pork with 2 Tbsp. dark soy, 1 tsp. sugar, ¼ tsp. gourmet powder, 1 tsp. cooking wine and drops of sesame seed oil.
2) HEAT WOK*, brown green onions, garlic and ginger, put in pork and saute for 1 minute. Add ½ C. water. Cover with lid and cook for 10 minutes.
3) Stir in bamboo shoots, cover with lid and cook for another 10 minutes.
4) Add sauce and bring to a boil. Serve hot in a casserole, if available.

*refer HOW TO p. 21

MU SHU PORK

INGREDIENTS:

½ lb. lean pork, shredded
4 Chinese mushrooms, soaked
  and shredded
½ C. bamboo shoots, shredded
1 carrot, shredded
2 C. cabbage, shredded
1 green onion, cut to 1" lengths
½ tsp. minced ginger
½ tsp. minced garlic
3 eggs, beaten
18 eggroll skins(steamed
  until softened)

SAUCE:

½ tsp. salt
1 tsp. sugar
2 Tbsp. dark soy
¼ tsp. gourmet powder
1 tsp. Chinese cooking wine
drops of sesame seed oil
¼ C. water
1 Tbsp. Wonder Powder

FOR SPREADING:
4 Tbsp. YAN'S hoi sin sauce

METHOD:

1) Marinate pork with 1 tsp. Wonder Powder, 2 Tbsp. light soy, 1 Tbsp. cooking wine and ½ tsp. sesame seed oil.
2) HEAT WOK*, with 1 Tbsp. oil, stir in egg and cook until softly set. Remove and set aside.
3) HEAT WOK*, brown green onion, garlic and ginger; put in pork and saute until meat changes color. Add vegetables and STIR FRY*.
4) Add sauce and cook until boil, return egg pieces and mix well. Transfer to a platter.
5) To serve, take one eggroll skin, spread on YAN'S hoi sin sauce, add 1-2 Tbsp. Mu Shu Pork, roll up and serve.

*refer HOW TO p. 21

HAM BALLS

INGREDIENTS:

1 lb. chicken meat, minced
4 oz. ham, cooked & minced
2 oz. bamboo shoots, minced
2 oz. water chestnuts, minced
4 green onions, chopped fine
½ tsp. minced garlic
1 C. YAN'S Almighty Powder

SEASONING:

½ tsp. salt
¼ tsp. gourmet powder
½ tsp. Chinese 5 spice powder
1 tsp. sugar
2 Tbsp. light soy sauce
1 Tbsp. Chinese cooking wine
2 Tbsp. YAN'S Wonder Powder
drops of sesame seed oil
dash pepper

METHOD:

1) Mix all ingredients (except YAN'S Almighty Powder) in a bowl. Stir until meat becomes condensed.
2) Form mixture into balls. Put into a steamer and steam for 10 minutes.
3) Prepare battermix by dissolving YAN'S Almighty Powder with an equal amount of water, and stirring until it forms a smooth consistency.
4) Place a few balls into battermix with a spoon and pick them out one at a time. Place them into hot oil and DEEP FRY* until golden brown. Drain and display on a plate garnished with shredded lettuce.

*refer HOW TO p. 21

CURRY SPARERIBS

INGREDIENTS:

1 lb. spareribs, cut to
  3" pieces
2 Tbsp. curry powder
½ tsp. Chinese 5 spice powder
1 tsp. minced garlic
1 Tbsp. light soy sauce

½ tsp. salt
¼ tsp. gourmet powder
1 tsp. sugar
1 Tbsp. Chinese cooking wine
2 Tbsp. YAN'S Wonder Powder
1 egg, beaten

METHOD:

1) Marinate spareribs with curry powder, minced garlic, gourmet powder, light soy sauce, Chinese 5 spice powder, sugar, salt and Chinese cooking wine.
2) Dip each spare rib in beaten egg and roll it in YAN'S Wonder Powder.
3) Heat 4 C. of peanut oil in a hot wok. DEEP FRY* spareribs at medium heat for about 10 minutes.
4) Display in a platter garnished with lettuce leaves.

*refer HOW TO p. 21

PORK WITH ZUCCHINI

INGREDIENTS:

6 oz. pork butt, sliced thinly
2 C. zucchini, sliced thinly
½ onion, wedged

BLACK BEAN PASTE:

2 tsp. salted black beans,
  rinsed and minced
1 Tbsp. green onion, chopped fine
1 tsp. minced garlic
1 tsp. minced ginger
1 tsp. oil
BLEND TOGETHER INTO A PASTE

SAUCE:

2 Tbsp. dark soy sauce
1 tsp. sugar
¼ tsp. gourmet powder
1 tsp. Chinese cooking wine
drops of sesame seed oil
1 Tbsp. Wonder Powder
¼ C. water

METHOD:

1) Marinate pork with 1 tsp. Wonder Powder, 2 Tbsp. light soy, 1 tsp. cooking wine and drops of sesame seed oil.
2) HEAT WOK*, brown black bean paste. Add pork and onions, saute until meat changes color. Add zucchini and STIR FRY*.
3) Add sauce and bring to a boil.

*refer HOW TO p. 21

PORK WITH CABBAGE

INGREDIENTS:

6 oz. pork butt, sliced
2 C. cabbage, shredded
1 green onion, cut to 1" lengths
½ tsp. minced ginger
½ tsp. minced garlic

SAUCE:

½ tsp. salt
1 tsp. light soy
¼ tsp. gourmet powder
1 tsp. Chinese cooking wine
drops sesame seed oil
1 Tbsp. Wonder Powder
½ tsp. sugar
⅓ C. water
1 Tbsp. oyster sauce

METHOD:

1) Marinate pork with 1 tsp. Wonder Powder, 1 Tbsp. light soy, 1 tsp. cooking wine and drops sesame seed oil.
2) HEAT WOK*, brown green onion, garlic and ginger. Put in pork and saute until meat changes color. Add vegetables and STIR FRY*.
3) Add sauce and bring to a boil.

*refer HOW TO p. 21

PORK WITH WALNUTS

INGREDIENTS:

8 oz. lean pork, diced to ½" pcs.
2 stalks celery, diced to ½" pcs.
½ C. fresh mushrooms, cut in half
1 carrot, diced to ¼" pcs., blanched
4 oz. roasted walnuts
3 green onions, cut 1" lengths
½ tsp. minced garlic
½ tsp. minced ginger

SAUCE:

2 Tbsp. hoi sin sauce
¼ tsp. Chinese 5 spice powder
1 tsp. Chinese cooking wine
drops of sesame seed oil
½ tsp. salt
½ tsp. gourmet powder
1 Tbsp. YAN'S Wonder Powder
1 Tbsp. oyster sauce
¼ C. water

METHOD:

1) Marinate pork in hoi sin sauce, Chinese cooking wine, light soy sauce, minced ginger and gourmet powder for half hour.
2) HEAT WOK*, put in minced garlic and pork pieces. Saute for 1 minute. Add vegetables and STIR FRY*.
3) Add sauce and bring to a boil. Add walnuts and serve.

*refer HOW TO p. 21

LION'S HEAD

INGREDIENTS:

1 lb. ground pork
2 green onions, chopped fine
1 tsp. minced ginger
½ tsp. minced garlic
1 egg, beaten
½ lb. Chinese cabbage,
    cut into 3" pieces
2 Tbsp. water chestnuts, minced

SAUCE:

3 Tbsp. light soy sauce
1 Tbsp. dark soy sauce
1 Tbsp. Chinese cooking wine
1½ Tbsp. YAN'S Wonder Powder
¼ tsp. gourmet powder
1 tsp. sugar
2 Tbsp. oyster sauce
¼ C. water
drops of sesame seed oil

PORK

METHOD:

1) Marinate pork with 1 tsp. salt, 1 tsp. sugar, 1 Tbsp. Chinese cooking wine, green onion, ginger, water chestnuts, egg and 2 Tbsp. Yan's Wonder Powder. Knead well and form into 4 large meatballs, set aside.
2) Coat outside of meatballs lightly with YAN'S Wonder Powder. Heat up 2 Cups oil and DEEP FRY* meatballs (to brown).
3) HEAT WOK*, add minced garlic and Chinese cabbage. Stir for ½ minute, then add ½ C. water or chicken soup stock. Place meatballs on top of cabbage. Cover with a lid and cook at medium heat for 15-20 minutes.
4) Add sauce and bring to a boil.

*refer HOW TO p. 21

PORK WITH BABY CORN

INGREDIENTS:

6 oz. lean pork, thinly sliced
1 C. baby corn
$1/3$ C. fresh mushrooms
$1/2$ onion, wedged
1 green onion, cut to 1" lengths
$1/2$ tsp. minced garlic
$1/2$ tsp. minced ginger

SAUCE:

$1/2$ tsp. salt
1 tsp. light soy
2 Tbsp. oyster sauce
$1/4$ tsp. gourmet powder
1 tsp. cooking wine
drops of sesame seed oil
1 Tbsp. Wonder Powder
$1/2$ tsp. sugar
$1/4$ C. water

METHOD:

1) Marinate pork with 1 tsp. Wonder Powder, 1 Tbsp. light soy, 1 tsp. cooking wine and drops of sesame seed oil.
2) HEAT WOK*, brown green onion, garlic and ginger; put in pork and onion and saute until meat changes color.
3) Add vegetables and STIR FRY*. Add sauce and bring to a boil.

*refer HOW TO p. 21

PORK WITH BEAN SPROUTS

INGREDIENTS:

6 oz. lean pork, shredded
3 C. bean sprouts
4 green onions, (green stem cut to 2" lengths-white part to 1" length)
$1/2$ carrot, finely shredded
$1/2$ tsp. minced ginger
$1/2$ tsp. minced garlic

SAUCE:

$1/2$ tsp. salt
2 Tbsp. oyster sauce
1 tsp. light soy
$1/4$ tsp. gourmet powder
1 tsp. Chinese cooking wine
drops of sesame seed oil
$1 1/2$ Tbsp. Wonder Powder
$1/2$ tsp. sugar
$1/4$ C. water

METHOD:

1) Marinate pork with 1 tsp. Wonder Powder, 1 Tbsp. light soy, 1 tsp. cooking wine and drops of sesame seed oil.
2) HEAT WOK*, brown white part of green onion, garlic and ginger; add pork and saute until meat changes colour. Add vegetables and STIR FRY*.
3) Add sauce and bring to a boil, stir in remainder of green onion.

*refer HOW TO p. 21

CHICKEN SLICES WITH PINEAPPLE

INGREDIENTS:

12 oz. chicken meat, sliced
8 oz. pineapple chunks
1 sm. green pepper, cut in squares
1 sm. red pepper, cut in squares
½ tsp. minced garlic
½ tsp. minced ginger
3 green onion, cut to 1" lengths

SAUCE:

½ tsp. Chinese cooking wine
¼ tsp. salt
¼ tsp. gourmet powder
1 Tbsp. YAN'S Wonder Powder
1 tsp. light soy sauce
drops of sesame seed oil
¼ C. water

METHOD:

1) Marinate chicken with Chinese cooking wine, light soy sauce and gourmet powder.
2) HEAT WOK*, brown green onion, garlic, ginger; add chicken and saute until meat changes color.
3) Put in all vegetables, ¼ tsp. salt and stir for 4 minutes.
4) When chicken is done, add sauce mixture and bring to a boil. Mix well and serve.

*refer HOW TO p. 21

CHICKEN IN GREEN BASKET

INGREDIENTS:

1 lb. chicken breast
20 pcs. cooked ham, sliced to
   ¾" x 2" strips
2 C. broccoli, flowerets
½ tsp. minced ginger
½ tsp. minced garlic
¼ tsp. baking soda
2 Tbsp. peanut oil

SAUCE:

¼ tsp. salt
½ tsp. sugar
¼ tsp. gourmet powder
1 tsp. Chinese cooking wine
2 Tbsp. oyster sauce
drops of sesame seed oil
1 Tbsp. Wonder Powder
¼ C. water (or chicken broth)

CHICKEN

METHOD:

1) Parboil chicken breasts in a wok with 4 C. water. Cover with a lid and cook for 10 minutes. Drain and set aside to cool. (Save chicken stock for making sauce).
2) Remove the meat from bone and cut into ½" x ¾" x 2" slices. (20 pcs.)
3) Arrange alternately 1 pc. chicken with 1 pc. ham on platter making about 3 rows. Steam for 5 minutes in wok.
4) Blanch broccoli in boiling water with 1 tsp. salt, 2 tsp. oil and ¼ tsp. baking soda for 3 minutes. Drain and arrange on edge of platter.
5) HEAT WOK*, put in sauce and bring to a boil. Pour sauce over chicken and ham slices.

*refer HOW TO p.21

LETTUCE WRAP CHICKEN

INGREDIENTS:

12 oz. chicken meat, minced
½ C. carrot, minced
½ C. water chestnuts, minced
1 onion, minced
6 Chinese mushrooms, soaked
  and minced
½ C. cooked ham, minced
2 Tbsp. green onion, chopped fine
½ tsp. minced garlic
½ tsp. minced ginger
1 head of lettuce

SAUCE:

½ tsp. salt
½ tsp. sugar
1 tsp. light soy
¼ tsp. gourmet powder
2 Tbsp. oyster sauce
1 Tbsp. Chinese cooking wine
drops of sesame seed oil
dash of pepper
1 Tbsp. Wonder Powder
¼ C. water

METHOD:

1) Marinate minced chicken with 1 Tbsp. Wonder Powder, 2 Tbsp. light soy, 1 Tbsp. cooking wine and drops of sesame seed oil.
2) Separate lettuce leaves, clean and keep in refrigerator for later use.
3) HEAT WOK*, brown green onion, garlic and ginger; put in minced chicken. Saute until meat changes color, remove and set aside.
4) STIR FRY* vegetables: return meat to wok. Add sauce and bring to a boil. Transfer to serving platter.
5) To serve, wrap, 1-2 Tbsp. chicken mixture in lettuce leaf. Dip in YAN'S hoi sin sauce. Serve.

*refer HOW TO p. 21

CHICKEN IN BLACK BEAN SAUCE

INGREDIENTS:

½ chicken, cut to bite size pcs.
½ C. green pepper, cut in
  triangular sections
½ C. onion, wedges
2 Tbsp. black beans, rinsed
1 tsp. minced ginger
1 tsp. minced garlic
1 tsp. minced green onion

SAUCE:

1 Tbsp. dark soy
½ tsp. salt
1 tsp. sugar
¼ tsp. gourmet powder
1 Tbsp. Chinese cooking wine
drops of sesame seed oil
1 Tbsp. Wonder Powder
¼ C. water

METHOD:

1) In a bowl, mix black beans, minced garlic, ginger and green onion. Use the handle of cleaver to crush this into a paste.
2) HEAT WOK*, brown black bean paste, add chicken and saute for 1 min. Add ¼ C. water, cover with lid and cook for 15 minutes.
3) Add vegetables and sauce, bring to a boil and serve hot.

*refer HOW TO p. 21

CHICKEN

CHICKEN WITH LYCHEE

INGREDIENTS:

12 oz. chicken meat sliced
1 C. lychee, drained
1 red pepper, cut in triangular
    sections
3 green onions, cut to 2" lengths
½ tsp. minced garlic
½ tsp. minced ginger

SAUCE:

1 Tbsp. sugar
3 Tbsp. tomato ketchup
½ C. syrup from lychee
 1 Tbsp. Wonder Powder
1 Tbsp. light soy

METHOD:

1) Marinate chicken with 1 Tbsp. Wonder Powder, 2 Tbsp. light soy, 1 Tbsp. Chinese cooking wine and drops of sesame seed oil.
2) HEAT WOK*, brown green onions, garlic and ginger; put in chicken, saute until meat changes color. Add pepper, onion, ½ tsp. salt, 2 Tbsp. water, cover with a lid and cook for 2 minutes.
3) Add sauce and bring to a boil. Put in lychee, mix well and serve hot.

*refer HOW TO p. 21

PAPER WRAPPED CHICKEN

INGREDIENTS:

8 oz. chicken meat, sliced
1/3 C. bamboo shoots
2 Tbsp. Chinese parsley (cut
    to 2" lengths)
2 green onions, cut to 2" lengths
20 sheets edible rice paper
    (or parchment paper)

SEASONING:

1 tsp. salt
1 tsp. sugar
1 tsp. light soy
2 Tbsp. oyster sauce
½ tsp. 5 spice powder
1 tsp. Chinese cooking wine
drops of sesame seed oil
dash white pepper
1 Tbsp. YAN'S Wonder Powder
2 Tbsp. peanut oil

CHICKEN

METHOD:

1) Marinate chicken and bamboo shoots with all the seasoning, Chinese parsley and green onion for 30 minutes.
2) Wrap 1 Tbsp. of marinated chicken in rice paper, fold up like an envelope and seal with egg.
3) DEEP FRY* with medium/high heat for 7-10 minutes. Drain and serve like an egg roll.
NOTE: If parchment paper is used, you will have to open the paper basket to serve the chicken.

*refer HOW TO p. 21

BABY CHICKEN DRUMSTICKS

INGREDIENTS:

16 chicken wings (cut tip off
  each wing)
¾ C. YAN'S Almighty Powder (dissolved in equal amount of water)
1 green onion, cut to 1" lengths
½ tsp. minced garlic
½ tsp. minced ginger

SAUCE:

¼ tsp. salt
1 Tbsp. YAN'S plum sauce
1 Tbsp. YAN'S hoi sin sauce
1 Tbsp. dark soy
drops of sesame seed oil
1 ½ Tbsp. Wonder Powder
½ C. water

METHOD:

1) Prepare chicken wing sticks by holding small end of bone, trim around
   with sharp knife to cut meat from bone. Then snap, and push meat
   down to large end. Using finger, pull skin and meat down over end of
   bone. They will resemble baby drumsticks.
2) Marinate chicken with 3 Tbsp. light soy, 1 tsp. Chinese 5 spice powder,
   2 Tbsp. Chinese cooking wine and drops of sesame seed oil.
3) Coat chicken sticks with batter and DEEP FRY* at medium/high heat
   until golden brown. Drain oil and set aside.
4) HEAT WOK*, brown green onions, garlic and ginger; put in sauce and
   bring to a boil. Add deep fried chicken sticks.

*refer HOW TO p. 21

PLUM SAUCE CHICKEN

INGREDIENTS:

12 oz. chicken meat, 1" cubes
½ head lettuce
1 C. YAN'S Almighty Powder
  dissolved in 1 C. water
½ tsp. Chinese 5 spice
drops sesame seed oil

SAUCE:

¹/₃ C. YAN'S plum sauce
1 Tbsp. vinegar
3 Tbsp. sugar
¼ C. water
½ tsp. minced ginger
½ tsp. minced garlic
1 Tbsp. Wonder Powder

METHOD:

1) Marinate chicken with 3 Tbsp. light soy, ½ tsp. 5 spice powder, 1 tsp.
   Chinese cooking wine and drops of sesame seed oil.
2) Heat oil in wok, coat chicken with batter and DEEP FRY* at medium-
   /heat until golden brown. Drain oil and transfer to a platter garnished
   with lettuce leaves.
3) HEAT WOK*, put in sauce and bring to boil, pour over chicken.

*refer HOW TO p. 21

SINGING CHICKEN CASSEROLE

INGREDIENTS:

1 lb. chicken meat, 1" cubes
4 Chinese mushrooms, soaked
   and cut in half
½ C. bamboo shoots, sliced
1 carrot, sliced
2 green onions, cut in 2" lengths
6 slices ginger
½ tsp. minced garlic

SAUCE:

½ tsp. salt
1 Tbsp. sugar
1 Tbsp. dark soy
2 Tbsp. oyster sauce
1 Tbsp. Chinese cooking wine
dash pepper
drops of sesame seed oil
½ C. water
1½ Tbsp. Wonder Powder

METHOD:

1) Heat 3 C. peanut oil for DEEP FRY*. Dust chicken with 3 Tbsp. YAN'S Wonder Powder and deep fry until golden brown.

2) HEAT WOK*, brown green onions, garlic and ginger. Put in parboiled chicken and all vegetables. Saute for 1 minute. Add ⅓ C. water, cover with lid and cook for 10 minutes. Add sauce and bring to boil.

3) Transfer to heat-proof casserole with lid. Heat casserole until sauce boils.

*refer HOW TO p. 21

PONG PONG CHICKEN

INGREDIENTS:

1 chicken breast
1 C. cucumber, peeled, cored
   and sliced
6 radishes for garnishing

DRESSING:

1 Tbsp. light soy
½ tsp. hot mustard (optional)
1 tsp. sugar
1 tsp. sesame seed oil
1 Tbsp. tobasco sauce (optional)
½ tsp. gourmet powder
1 tsp. minced green onion
½ tsp. minced ginger
½ tsp. minced garlic
2 Tbsp. peanut butter in
        4 Tbsp. water

CHICKEN

METHOD:

1) Parboil chicken in a wok with 4 C. water for 15 mins. Drain and let cool.
2) Pound chicken meat with a meat tenderizer and tear to small slivers.
3) Display cucumber slices on a platter and place chicken meat on top.
4) Mix dressing well and pour on top of chicken. Serve.

HOI SIN CHICKEN

INGREDIENTS:

2 lb. chicken, chopped to
    bite-size pieces
4 oz. water chestnuts
1 tsp. minced ginger
½ tsp. minced garlic
1 C. broccoli, flowerets
½ C. carrot, slices
1 sm. onion, shredded
¼ C. YAN'S Almighty Powder
¼ tsp. Chinese 5 spice powder
2 Tbsp. Chinese cooking wine

SAUCE:

4 Tbsp. hoi sin sauce
1 Tbsp. dark soy sauce
1 Tbsp. sugar
1 tsp. Chinese cooking wine
drops of sesame seed oil
1 ½ Tbsp. Wonder Powder
½ C. water

METHOD:

1) Sprinkle chicken with Chinese 5 spice and ½ tsp. salt. Coat lightly with YAN'S Almighty Powder. DEEP FRY* until golden brown, remove & drain.
2) HEAT WOK*, fry ginger, garlic and onion for 1 minute, add broccoli, carrots, water chestnuts, gourmet powder and Chinese cooking wine. STIR FRY* for 1 minute. Add sauce and bring to a boil.
3) Add chicken to vegetables and sauce, toss over at high heat for 2 mins.

*refer HOW TO p. 21

SOY SAUCE CHICKEN

INGREDIENTS:

½ roasting chicken OR
    4 chicken legs
6 Chinese mushrooms, soaked
    and cut in half
2 green onion, cut to 2" lengths
½ tsp. minced garlic
½ tsp. minced ginger

SAUCE:

¼ C. dark soy
2 Tbsp. light soy
2 Tbsp. sugar
¼ tsp. gourmet powder
1 Tbsp. Chinese cooking wine
drops of sesame seed oil
1 C. water

METHOD:

1) Marinate chicken with 1 Tbsp. Wonder Powder, 2 Tbsp. light soy, 1 Tbsp. cooking wine and drops of sesame seed oil.
2) DEEP FRY* chicken until brown. Drain and set aside.
3) HEAT WOK*, brown green onion, garlic and ginger; put in chicken, mushrooms and sauce. Cover with lid and simmer for 15 mins at medium heat. Stir occasionally.
4) Cut chicken into chunks, display on a platter. Pour sauce over chicken.

*refer HOW TO p. 21

CURRIED CHICKEN

INGREDIENTS:

1 whole chicken, cut to 1 ½" pcs.
1 lg. potato, cut in sm. sections
1 lg. onion, wedged
1 green pepper, cut in sections
1 tsp. minced garlic
1 tsp. minced ginger
1 tsp. minced green onion
2 Tbsp. curry powder

SAUCE:

1 tsp. sugar
½ tsp. gourmet powder
2 Tbsp. curry powder
¼ C. cream
½ C. water
1 ½ Tbsp. Wonder Powder

METHOD:

1) Marinate chicken with 4 Tbsp. light soy, 2 Tbsp. Chinese cooking wine and 1 tsp. Chinese 5 spice powder.
2) HEAT WOK*, brown green onion, garlic, ginger with curry powder. Put in chicken, potato, and onion and saute for 1-2 minutes. Add ½ C. water, cover with lid and cook at medium heat for 20-30 minutes.
3) Add green pepper and sauce and bring to a boil.

*refer HOW TO p. 21

CHICKEN WITH PEACHES

INGREDIENTS:

1 lb. chicken meat, cut to 1" cubes
1 C. peaches (quarters)
½ tsp. salt
²/₃ C. YAN'S Almighty Powder
  (dissolved in ²/₃ C. water and
  drops of oil)
½ tsp. gourmet powder
½ tsp. minced garlic
1 green pepper, cut in triangular
  sections

SAUCE:

½ tsp. salt
2 Tbsp. lemon juice
1 Tbsp. sugar
½ C. syrup from canned peaches
1 ½ Tbsp. Wonder Powder

METHOD:

1) Marinate chicken with 4 Tbsp. light soy, 1 Tbsp. cooking wine, 1 tsp. Chinese 5 spice powder, ½ tsp. salt, ½ tsp. gourmet powder and drops of sesame seed oil.
2) Coat chicken with batter and DEEP FRY* at medium/high heat until golden brown. Drain oil and set aside.
3) HEAT WOK*, brown garlic, green pepper for ½ minute. Add sauce mixture and bring to a boil. Return deep fried chicken and peaches to wok. Mix and serve.

*refer HOW TO p. 21

CHICKEN

CHICKEN WITH WALNUTS

INGREDIENTS:

1 lb. chicken meat, cut
  ½" cubes
½ tsp. minced ginger
½ tsp. minced garlic
1 sm. chili pepper (optional)
4 oz. roasted walnuts
1 sm. green pepper, cut
  small squares
1 sm. red pepper, cut small squares
3 green onion, cut 1" lengths

SAUCE:

1½ Tbsp. Wonder Powder dissolved
  in ¼ C. water
1 tsp. sugar
1 Tbsp. oyster sauce
few drops tobasco (optional)
drops of sesame seed oil
1 tsp. cooking wine

METHOD:

1) Marinate chicken with 2 Tbsp. light soy sauce, 1 tsp. Chinese cooking
   wine and drops of sesame seed oil.
2) HEAT WOK*, brown onion, garlic and ginger. Add chicken and saute for
   2 minutes, add all vegetables and STIR FRY*.
3) Add sauce and bring to a boil. Put in walnuts and mix well.

*refer HOW TO p. 21

CHICKEN WITH SNOW PEAS

INGREDIENTS:

12 oz. chicken meat, slivers
1½ C. snow peas
1 onion, wedged
¼ C. carrot, sliced
2 Tbsp. black beans, rinsed and
  minced
1 tsp. minced ginger
1 tsp. minced garlic

SAUCE:

½ tsp. salt
1 Tbsp. oyster sauce
½ tsp. sugar
¼ tsp. gourmet powder
1 Tbsp. Wonder Powder
1 tsp. Chinese cooking wine
drops of sesame seed oil
¼ C. water

METHOD:

1) Marinate chicken with 1 Tbsp. Wonder Powder, 2 Tbsp. light soy, 1
   Tbsp. Chinese cooking wine, and drops sesame seed oil.
2) HEAT WOK*, brown ginger and garlic; add chicken slivers and saute
   until meat changes color. Remove and set aside.
3) In same wok, STIR FRY* vegetables; return meat to wok. Add sauce
   and bring to a boil.

*refer HOW TO p. 21

PINEAPPLE HONEY CHICKEN BALLS

INGREDIENTS:

2 lb. fryer chicken, cut to
   bite-size pieces
1 Tbsp. minced ginger
½ tsp. minced garlic
10 oz. pineapple chunks
1 green pepper, cut to 1" squares
1 carrot, sliced
4 green onions, cut to 1" lengths
1 C. YAN'S Almighty Powder

SAUCE:

2 Tbsp. honey
drops of sesame seed oil
¼ tsp. gourmet powder
2 Tbsp. dark soy
1 Tbsp. Chinese cooking wine
1 ½ Tbsp. Wonder Powder
⅓ C. water

METHOD:

1) Marinate chicken with ½ tsp. 5 spice powder, 1 tsp. salt and Yan's almighty powder diluted with ⅔ C. water.
2) DEEP FRY* chicken until golden brown; remove and drain on paper towel.
3) Remove oil from wok except for 2 Tbsp. Use high heat to cook ginger, garlic and onion for 1 minute. Add pineapple, carrot and green pepper. Add sauce. Bring to a boil then add to chicken.

*refer HOW TO p. 21

BEAN SPROUTS WITH CHICKEN

INGREDIENTS:

8 oz. chicken meat, sliced
1 tsp. YAN'S Wonder Powder
2 C. bean sprouts, fresh
1 C. celery, shredded
½ C. carrot, shredded
1 sm. onion, shredded
3 green onions, cut to 1" lengths
½ tsp. minced ginger

SAUCE:

2 tsp. light soy sauce
drops of sesame seed oil
1 tsp. oyster sauce
½ tsp. sugar
1 Tbsp. Wonder Powder
¼ C. water

CHICKEN

METHOD:

1) Marinate chicken with 1 tsp. Chinese cooking wine, 1 tsp. Wonder Powder and 1 Tbsp. light soy sauce for 5 minutes.
2) HEAT WOK*, brown minced ginger, green onion and onion. Add chicken and STIR FRY* until meat changes color.
3) Add bean sprouts, celery, carrot and ½ tsp. of salt to chicken mixture. Stir mix, cover with a lid and cook at high heat for 2-3 mins.
4) Add sauce, bring to a boil and mix well.

*refer HOW TO p. 21

KUNG PAO CHICKEN

INGREDIENTS:

12 oz. chicken meat, diced
½ C. cucumber, diced
½ C. carrot, diced
½ C. peanuts, roasted
2 green onions, cut to 1" lengths
½ tsp. minced ginger
½ tsp. minced garlic

SAUCE:

1 tsp. sugar
¼ tsp. gourmet powder
1 Tbsp. tobasco sauce
2 Tbsp. dark soy
drops of sesame seed oil
1 Tbsp. Wonder Powder
¼ C. water

METHOD:

1) Marinate chicken with 1 Tbsp. Wonder Powder, 1 Tbsp. light soy, 1 Tbsp. Chinese cooking wine and drops of sesame seed oil.
2) HEAT WOK*, brown green onion, garlic and ginger; put in chicken and saute until meat changes color. Remove and set aside.
3) STIR FRY* vegetables in same wok, return meat and add sauce. Bring to a boil and serve hot.

*refer HOW TO p. 21

SPICY CHICKEN

INGREDIENTS:

1 lb. chicken meat, sliced
4 stalks, green onion, cut to
    2" lengths
½ tsp. minced ginger
1 Tbsp. minced garlic
4 oz. roasted peanuts, unsalted

SAUCE:

½ tsp. black pepper
½ tsp. salt
1 ½ tsp. sugar
¼ tsp. gourmet powder
1 Tbsp. tobasco sauce
2 Tbsp. dark soy
1 Tbsp. Chinese cooking wine
drops of sesame seed oil
1 Tbsp. Wonder Powder
¼ C. water

METHOD:

1) Marinate chicken with 1 Tbsp. Wonder Powder, 2 Tbsp. light soy, 1 Tbsp. cooking wine and 1 tsp. sesame seed oil.
2) HEAT WOK*, brown green onions, garlic and ginger; put in chicken and saute until meat changes color. Add sauce and bring to boil. Add peanuts, mix well.

*refer HOW TO p. 21

CHICKEN

CHICKEN IN OYSTER SAUCE

INGREDIENTS:

1 lb. chicken meat, shredded
¾ C. straw mushrooms
4 Chinese mushrooms, soaked
   and shredded
2 green onions, cut to 2" lengths
½ tsp. minced ginger
½ tsp. minced garlic
4 oz. Rice vermicelli

SAUCE:

1 tsp. sugar
1 Tbsp. dark soy
2 Tbsp. oyster sauce
1 ½ Tbsp. Wonder Powder
drops sesame seed oil
1 Tbsp. Chinese cooking wine
1/3 C. water

METHOD:

1) Marinate chicken with 1 Tbsp. Wonder Powder, 2 Tbsp. light soy, 1 Tbsp. cooking wine and drops of sesame seed oil.
2) Heat 2 C. of peanut oil in wok. When it is very hot, DEEP FRY* rice vermicelli until puffed up. Drain and display on platter.
3) HEAT WOK*, brown green onion, garlic and ginger; put in chicken and saute until meat changes color. Remove and set aside.
4) Using same wok, STIR FRY* vegetables, return meat to wok. Add sauce and bring to boil. Transfer chicken to bed of deep fried vermicelli.

*refer HOW TO p. 21

SWEET AND HOT CHICKEN

INGREDIENTS:

1 whole chicken, cut up to
   serving pieces
1 C. YAN'S Almighty Powder
   (dissolved in 1 C. water)
3 green onions, cut to 2" lengths
½ tsp. minced ginger
½ tsp. minced garlic

SAUCE:

½ tsp. salt
1 Tbsp. sugar
2 Tbsp. honey
1 Tbsp. Tobasco sauce
1 Tbsp. lemon juice
1/3 C. water
1 ½ Tbsp. Wonder Powder

METHOD:

1) Marinate chicken with 4 Tbsp. light soy, 1 tsp. 5 spice powder, 2 Tbsp. Chinese cooking wine and drops of sesame seed oil.
2) Coat chicken with batter and DEEP FRY* at medium/high heat until golden brown. Drain oil and set aside.
3) HEAT WOK*, brown green onion, ginger and garlic. Add sauce and bring to a boil. Return chicken to wok and mix well.

*refer HOW TO p. 21

CHICKEN

CHICKEN ROLL

INGREDIENTS:

2 chicken breasts, deboned and
   cut into 4 pieces
4 slices cooked ham
4-6 egg roll skin

$^2/_3$ C. YAN'S Almighty Powder
1 C. lettuce, shredded
1 clove garlic, minced

METHOD:

1)   Use a meat tenderizer and pound chicken pieces until they become thin.
2)   Boil chicken in 1 C. water, 1 tsp. salt, 1 Tbsp. light soy, ½ tsp. 5 spice powder, dash pepper and drops of sesame seed oil for 15 minutes.
3)   Prepare battermix by dissolving YAN'S Almighty Powder with equal amount of water, stirring until smooth.
4)   Place ham on chicken, then place diagonally on top of egg roll skin. Fold up both ends and roll egg rolls clockwise.
5)   Heat oil in wok for deep frying. Coat chicken rolls with batter, DEEP FRY* at medium/high heat until golden brown. Drain and cut into 1" diagonal slices, place on plate garnished with shredded lettuce.

*refer HOW TO p. 21

SWEET & SOUR DRUMSTICKS

INGREDIENTS:

6-8 sm. chicken drumsticks
¼ tsp. gourmet powder
2 Tbsp. light soy sauce
$^2/_3$ C. YAN'S Almighty Powder
1 egg, beaten
½ tsp. minced ginger
1 Tbsp. YAN'S Wonder Powder
1 small green pepper, shredded
1 small red pepper, shredded
½ C. pineapple chunks

SAUCE:

$^1/_3$ C. water
½ C. sugar
2 Tbsp. tomato paste
1 Tbsp. light soy
1 Tbsp. Wonder Powder
1 Tbsp. vinegar

METHOD:

1)   Marinate chicken with gourmet powder, ginger, light soy for 10 minutes.
2)   Steam drumsticks at high heat for 10 minutes.
3)   Dip chicken in beaten egg and roll in Almighty Powder. DEEP FRY* until golden brown.
4)   HEAT WOK*, saute pepper for 1 minute. Add sauce and bring to boil. Add pineapple and chicken. Mix well.

*refer HOW TO p. 21

BEGGAR'S CHICKEN

INGREDIENTS:

1 whole fryer chicken (3 lb.)
½ C. bamboo shoots, sliced
½ C. cellophane vermicelli,
   soaked 2 hrs. and cut to
   2" lengths
3 green onions, cut to 2" lengths
½ tsp. minced garlic
½ tsp. minced ginger
2 Tbsp. lard

FOR CLAY DOUGH:

5 C. flour
2½ lbs. salt
2 C. water

SEASONING:

1 Tbsp. peanut oil
1 tsp. salt
1 tsp. sugar
1 Tbsp. light soy sauce
½ tsp. gourmet powder
drops of sesame seed oil
dash pepper
1 Tbsp. Wonder Powder
2 Tbsp. water
1 Tbsp. Chinese cooking wine

METHOD:

1) Marinate chicken by rubbing it with a mixture of 3 Tbsp. dark soy sauce, 1 tsp. salt, 1 Tbsp. sugar, 1 Tbsp. water, drops of sesame seed oil and ½ tsp. 5-spice powder.

2) Prepare filling by mixing bamboo shoots, cellophane vermicelli, green onion, ginger, and garlic with the seasoning. Fill in chicken cavity and secure end with skewer.

3) Prepare clay dough by mixing flour and salt with water. The dough should not be too soft, otherwise it will be hard to handle.

4) Smear lard over one large piece of aluminum foil. Wrap around chicken and secure like a parcel.

5) Roll dough out to about ½" thickness, fold dough over the chicken parcel. Press edges together. Make sure there are no holes in the pastry.

6) Place chicken on oiled baking sheet and bake in hot oven for 450°F for 1 hour. Reduce to medium heat of 300°F and bake for 3 more hours.

7) Use hammer to help break away the pastry clay. Remove chicken from foil and arrange on platter to serve.

CHICKEN

BANANA CHICKEN

INGREDIENTS:

1 large banana cut diagonally into 10 pieces	¼ tsp. gourmet powder
1 minced chicken meat	drops of sesame seed oil
1 Tbsp. green onion, chopped	1 Tbsp. light soy sauce
1 egg, beaten	2 tsp. oyster sauce
½ C. bread crumbs	½ tsp. sugar
	¼ tsp. Chinese five spice
	2 Tbsp. Wonder Powder

METHOD:

1) Mix meat with all ingredients except bread crumbs.
2) Wrap banana with chicken mixture. Roll in bread crumbs.
3) DEEP FRY* in hot oil until golden brown.

*refer HOW TO p. 21

CHICKEN WITH MUSHROOMS
(Moo Goo Gai Pin)

INGREDIENTS:

12 oz. chicken meat, sliced
1 C. fresh mushrooms
⅓ C. bamboo shoots, sliced
⅓ C. onion, wedged
1 green onion, cut to 1" lengths
½ tsp. minced ginger
½ tsp. minced garlic
¼ C. green pepper, cut to 1" squares
drops sesame seed oil

SAUCE:

½ tsp. salt
1 Tbsp. dark soy
1 tsp. sugar
2 Tbsp. oyster sauce
dash pepper
1 Tbsp. Chinese cooking wine
drops of sesame seed oil
¼ C. water
1 Tbsp. Wonder Powder

METHOD:

1) Marinate chicken with 1 Tbsp. Wonder Powder, 2 Tbsp. light soy, 1 Tbsp. cooking wine and drops sesame seed oil.
2) HEAT WOK*, brown green onion, garlic and ginger, put in chicken and sauté until meat changes colour.
3) Add vegetables and STIR FRY* for 3-4 minutes. Add sauce and cook until it boils.

*refer HOW TO p. 21

ORANGE CHICKEN WINGS

INGREDIENTS:

12 chicken wings, cut into sections
2 oranges, sliced
½ tsp. garlic, minced
½ tsp. ginger, minced
2 green onion, cut to 1"
1 sm. onion, wedged

SAUCE:

½ tsp. salt
1 Tbsp. sugar
1 Tbsp. dark soy
1 tsp. cooking wine
$^1/_3$ C. water
1 Tbsp. Wonder Powder

METHOD:

1) Blanch chicken wings in boiling water for 2 minutes.
2) HEAT WOK*, brown green onion, garlic, and ginger; put in chicken wings and orange. Saute for 5 minutes. Add sauce mixture (except Wonder Powder) and cook for 10 minutes. Thicken sauce with Wonder Powder.

*refer HOW TO p. 21

HOT PEPPER CHICKEN

INGREDIENTS:

10 oz. chicken meat, diced
1 green pepper, diced
1 red pepper, diced
1 sm. onion, diced
1 green onion, cut to 1" lengths
½ tsp. minced garlic
½ tsp. minced ginger

SAUCE:

¼ tsp. salt
1 tsp. sugar
1 Tbsp. tobasco sauce
1 Tbsp. dark soy
1 Tbsp. oyster sauce
¼ tsp. gourmet powder
¼ C. water
1 Tbsp. Wonder Powder
1 tsp. cooking wine
drops of sesame seed oil

METHOD:

1) Marinate chicken with 1 tsp. Wonder Powder, 2 Tbsp. light soy, 1 Tbsp. cooking wine and drops sesame seed oil.
2) HEAT WOK*, brown green onion, garlic and ginger; put in chicken and saute until meat changes color. Add vegetables and STIR FRY*.
3) Add sauce and heat until boiling. Serve hot.

*refer HOW TO p. 21

CHICKEN

CHICKEN WITH CHESTNUTS

INGREDIENTS:
2 lb. chicken, cut into chunks
1 C. chestnuts, shelled, soaked
  for half day
3 green onions, cut to 1" lengths
1 tsp. ginger, minced
½ tsp. garlic, minced

SAUCE:
½ tsp. salt
2 Tbsp. dark soy
1 Tbsp. oyster sauce
1 tsp. sugar
1 tsp. cooking wine
drops of sesame seed oil
½ C. water

FOR THICKENING:
2 Tbsp. Wonder Powder
$1/3$ C. water

METHOD:
1) Marinate chicken with 1 Tbsp. Wonder Powder, 5 Tbsp. dark soy sauce, and 1 Tbsp. cooking wine.
2) Heat 4 C. peanut oil and DEEP FRY* chicken until golden brown. Drain and set aside.
3) HEAT WOK* brown green onion, garlic and ginger; put in chicken and chestnuts, saute for 1 miniute. Add sauce, cover with a lid and cook for 15 minutes. Stir in Wonder Powder to thicken sauce.

*refer HOW TO p. 21

CHICKEN WITH ONION SAUCE

INGREDIENTS:
1 lb. chicken meat
4 green onion, finely shredded
6 slices ginger, shredded
½ tsp. minced garlic
1 C. broccoli, flowerets

SAUCE:
½ tsp. salt
½ tsp. sugar
¼ tsp. gourmet powder
$2/3$ C. chicken broth
drops of sesame seed oil
1 ½ Tbsp. Wonder Powder

METHOD:
1) Boil chicken meat in wok with ½ tsp. salt. When done, remove and cut into 1 ½" cubes. Arrange on platter.
2) Using the chicken broth, boil broccoli, drain and garnish chicken.
3) Put ginger strips and shredded green onion on top of chicken. Heat up 2 Tbsp. oil until smoking. Pour over ginger and green onion.
4) HEAT WOK*, put in sauce and bring to boil. Pour over chicken before serving.

*refer HOW TO p. 21

CHICKEN

SWEET & SOUR CHICKEN BALLS

INGREDIENTS:

1 lb. chicken meat, cubed
1 C. YAN'S Almighty Powder
   dissolved in ¾ C. water
2 stalks celery, shredded
1 carrot, shredded
1 small onion, shredded
1 green pepper, shredded

SAUCE:

1 Tbsp. light soy
½ C. sugar
$^1/_3$ C. vinegar
½ C. water
2 Tbsp. tomato paste
1 Tbsp. Wonder Powder
¼ C. water

METHOD:

1) Marinate chicken with 2 Tbsp. light soy, ½ tsp. 5 spice powder, 1 Tbsp. cooking wine and drops sesame seed oil.
2) Coat chicken with batter (Almighty Powder & water) and DEEP FRY* at medium/high heat until golden brown. Drain oil and set aside.
3) HEAT WOK*, saute vegetables for ½ minute. Add sauce and bring to a boil. Return deep fried chicken and mix well.

*refer HOW TO p. 21

STUFFED CHICKEN WINGS

INGREDIENTS:

12 chicken wings
12 pcs. cooked ham (cut into
   1 ½" lengths)
4 green onions, cut to 1 ½" lengths
12 bamboo shoots,
   cut to 1 ½" lengths
1 egg white
$^2/_3$ C. YAN'S Almighty Powder

¼ tsp. gourmet powder
1 Tbsp. light soy sauce
drops of sesame seed oil
pinch Chinese 5 spice powder

CHICKEN

METHOD:

1) Cut tips and small drumsticks off each chicken wing. Use only the middle portion of the wing for stuffing. Drop into boiling water and cook for 5 minutes. Remove and drain.
2) Debone chicken wing by pushing the bone from one end, through the opposite end.
3) Insert strips of ham, green onion and bamboo shoots in the cavity. Marinate stuffed wings with drops of sesame seed oil, gourmet powder, and Chinese 5-spice powder.
4) Dissolve $^2/_3$ C. Almighty Powder with equal amount of water to form a smooth consistency. Dip chicken wings into battermix individually and DEEP FRY* until golden brown. (Serve with plum sauce or sweet & sour sauce).

*refer HOW TO p. 21

BEEF TENDERLOIN TEPPAN

INGREDIENTS:

1 lb. sirloin steak, cut
   to ¼" cubes
2 Tbsp. YAN'S Wonder Powder
¼ C. carrot, sliced
1 stalk broccoli, cut in
   bite size pieces
1 sm. onion, shredded
½ tsp. minced ginger
1 tsp. minced garlic

SAUCE:

1 Tbsp. Chinese cooking wine
pinch gourmet powder
pinch Chinese 5 spice powder
3 Tbsp. light soy sauce
2 Tbsp. tomato paste
3 Tbsp. HP Sauce
2 Tbsp. sugar
1 ½ Tbsp. Wonder Powder
½ C. water

METHOD:

1) Marinate beef cubes in dash gourmet powder, dash 5 spice powder, 2 Tbsp. light soy sauce, 1 Tbsp. Chinese cooking wine and 1 Tbsp. Wonder Powder for 30 minutes.
2) Heat 1 cup of oil in wok. Put in beef cubes and fry for 2 minutes until meat changes color. Remove from oil and drain.
3) Clean and HEAT WOK*. Add ginger, garlic and onion, saute for half minute. Then add all other vegetables and saute for 2 minutes.
4) Add sauce mix. Return beef and bring to a boil. (Serve on cast iron teppan, if possible).

*refer HOW TO p. 21

BEEF ROLLS

INGREDIENTS:

7 oz. beef, thinly sliced across
   the grain into 4 pieces
½ carrot, shredded
4 green onion, cut to 2" lengths
1 red pepper, shredded
2 Chinese mushrooms, soaked
   and shredded
1 tsp. minced ginger

SAUCE:

1 Tbsp. light soy
1 Tbsp. dark soy
1 Tbsp. sugar
¹/₃ C. water
1 Tbsp. oyster sauce
1 Tbsp. Wonder Powder
drops of sesame seed oil
dash pepper

METHOD:

1) Marinate beef with 3 Tbsp. dark soy, 1 tsp. minced ginger, 1 Tbsp. Chinese cooking wine, drops sesame seed oil, 1 Tbsp. Wonder Powder, 1 tsp. sugar and dash pepper.
2) Place shredded vegetables on middle of beef slice. Roll up and secure with toothpick. Make 4 rolls.
3) Heat oil in wok and DEEP FRY* beef rolls at medium/high heat until brown. Drain oil and cut in 1" sections, transfer to platter.
4) HEAT WOK*, add sauce and bring to a boil. Pour over beef rolls.

*refer HOW TO p. 21

CHICKEN SLICES WITH PINEAPPLE (page 73)

PRAWNS WITH MUSHROOMS (page 48)

HOT PEPPER CHICKEN (page 87)

PRAWNS WITH RAINBOW SAUCE (page 41)

CHICKEN WITH PEACHES (page 79)

SEAFOOD IN A NEST (page 49)

GOLD COIN BEEF (page 92)

SCALLOP DELIGHT (page 45)

SEA FESTIVAL TEPPAN (page 43)

SHRIMP IN BLACK BEAN SAUCE (page 29)

SPONGE CAKE (page 110)

PAPER WRAP BEEF (page 95)

PORK STUFFED CUCUMBERS (page 63)

BEEF WITH CELLOPHANE NOODLES (page 96)

SIU MAI (page 106)

BEEF TENDERLOIN TEPPAN (page 90)

BEEF STUFFED MUSHROOMS

INGREDIENTS:

12 large whole fresh mushrooms
(remove stems)
½ C. ground beef
2 green onion, chopped fine
¼ C. water chestnuts, (or
bamboo shoots) chopped fine
1 egg yoke
½ C. YAN'S Almighty Powder dissolved in ½ C. water, drops of
sesame seed oil

SEASONING:

½ tsp. salt
1 tsp. sugar
2 tsp. light soy sauce
1 Tbsp. oyster sauce
½ tsp. 5 spice powder
1 tsp. Chinese cooking wine
dash pepper
drops of sesame seed oil
¼ tsp. gourmet powder
2 Tbsp. Wonder Powder

METHOD:

1) Prepare stuffing by mixing and kneading beef, with onion, water chestnuts, egg yoke and all seasoning.

2) With a teaspoon, spread 1 tsp. of mixture evenly into cavity of each
mushroom.

3) Heat up 3 cups of oil in wok, dust filling with Wonder Powder, coat
mushroom with battermix and deep fry at medium heat until golden
brown. Serve with worchestershire sauce.

HONEY BEEF

INGREDIENTS:

1 lb. beef, sliced
1 green onion, chopped fine
½ tsp. minced garlic
½ tsp. minced ginger
3 Tbsp. YAN'S Almighty Powder
1 egg

SAUCE:

2 Tbsp. honey
2 Tbsp. water
¼ tsp. salt
1 Tbsp. oyster sauce
1 Tbsp. Wonder Powder

METHOD:

1) Marinate beef with 1 egg, 3 Tbsp. YAN'S Almighty Powder, 3 Tbsp. light
soy sauce, ¼ tsp. 5 spice powder, 1 Tbsp. cooking wine and drops
sesame seed oil.

2) DEEP FRY* beef at medium/high heat until golden brown. Drain oil and
set aside.

3) HEAT WOK*, add sauce and bring to a boil, stir in beef and mix well.

BEEF

*refer HOW TO p, 21

BEEF WITH CASHEW NUTS

INGREDIENTS:

12 oz. beef, cubed
6 oz. cashew nuts, roasted
½ C. celery, diced
½ C. water chestnuts, diced
½ C. baby sweet corn, cut to
   4 sections
¼ C. carrot, diced
½ tsp. minced garlic
3 green onion, cut to 1" lengths

SAUCE:

2 Tbsp. oyster sauce
1 Tbsp. light soy sauce
1 tsp. sugar
dash pepper
1 tsp. cooking wine
drops of sesame seed oil
1 Tbsp. Wonder Powder
¼ C. water

METHOD:

1) Marinate beef in Chinese cooking wine, 1 Tbsp. YAN'S Wonder Powder, light soy sauce, pepper and drops of sesame seed oil.
2) HEAT WOK*, brown garlic, green onion, add beef and saute until meat changes color. Remove and set aside.
3) HEAT WOK*, STIR FRY* all vegetables, when done, add sauce and bring to a boil. Add cashew nuts and mix well.

*refer How to p. 21

GOLD COIN BEEF

INGREDIENTS:

1 lb. beef tenderloin, sliced across
   grain to ¼" thickness
¼ C. green peas
1 med. onion, shredded
¼ tsp. minced garlic

SAUCE:

1 Tbsp. light soy sauce
3 Tbsp. sugar
2 Tbsp. tomato paste
⅓ C. water
1 Tbsp. Wonder Powder
¼ C. orange juice

BEEF

METHOD:

1) Marinate beef with ½ tsp. baking soda, 1 tsp. sugar, ½ tsp. salt, 1 tsp. sesame seed oil and 1 Tbsp. Chinese cooking wine for 2 hours.
2) Heat peanut oil in wok and DEEP FRY* beef for 1 minute. Remove and drain.
3) Retain 2 Tbsp. of oil in wok, reheat and add garlic and onion. Cook at high heat for 1 minute then add beef, green peas and stir mix for 2 minutes. Add sauce and bring to a boil. Serve over noodles.

*refer HOW TO p. 21

SHREDDED BEEF AND ONION

INGREDIENTS:

12 oz. beef, shredded
2 onions, shredded
½ tsp. minced garlic
½ tsp. minced ginger
2 green onions, cut to 2" lengths

SAUCE:

¼ tsp. salt
1 tsp. sugar
1 Tbsp. oyster sauce
¼ tsp. gourmet powder
1 Tbsp. Chinese cooking wine
drops of sesame seed oil
1 Tbsp. Wonder Powder
dash pepper
¼ C. water

METHOD:

1) Marinate beef with 1 tsp. Wonder Powder, 2 Tbsp. light soy, 1 Tbsp. cooking wine and drops of sesame seed oil.
2) HEAT WOK*, brown garlic, ginger and onions; add beef and saute until meat changes color.
3) Add sauce and bring to a boil. Serve hot.

*refer HOW TO p. 21

DEEP FRIED MEAT BALLS

INGREDIENTS:

½ C. YAN'S Almighty Powder
12 oz. ground beef
4 oz. ground pork
1 green onion, minced
dash pepper
½ tsp. gourmet powder
1 tsp. Chinese cooking wine

½ tsp. salt
½ tsp. sugar
¼ tsp. 5 spice powder
1 egg, beaten
drops of sesame seed oil
1 Tbsp. Wonder Powder
1 Tbsp. oyster sauce

METHOD:

1) Marinate meat with all ingredients and knead well for about 10 minutes. Form into balls approx. 1" diameter. Place on greased platter and steam for 10 minutes at high heat.
2) Dissolve ½ C. Almighty Powder in ½ C. water and drops of cooking oil. Dip meat balls into battermix and DEEP FRY* until golden brown. Place on bed of shredded lettuce and serve with plum sauce or spicy salt.

*refer HOW TO p. 21

BEEF

HOI SIN BEEF

INGREDIENTS:

1 lb. beef steak, cubed to 1"
¼ C. broccoli, flowerets
¼ C. baby corn
1 green onion, cut to 1" lengths
½ tsp. minced ginger
½ tsp. minced garlic

SAUCE:

1 Tbsp. dark soy
½ tsp. salt
2 Tbsp. hoi sin sauce
1 Tbsp. vinegar
1 Tbsp. sugar
⅓ C. water
1 Tbsp. Wonder Powder

METHOD:

1) Marinate beef cubes with 1 Tbsp. Wonder Powder, 3 Tbsp. light soy, 1 Tbsp. cooking wine and drops of sesame seed oil.
2) Heat up 2 C. oil, deep fry beef cubes until color changes to brown, remove and drain oil.
3) HEAT WOK*, brown green onion, garlic and ginger; STIR FRY* vegetables; return meat to wok. Add sauce and bring to a boil. Serve hot.

*refer HOW TO p. 21

GINGER BEEF CASSEROLE

INGREDIENTS:

1 lb. beef meat, sliced
4 green onions, cut to 2" lengths
1 Tbsp. ginger, shredded
½ tsp. minced garlic
4 oz. water chestnuts, sliced
¼ C. onion, shredded

SAUCE:

¼ tsp. salt
2 Tbsp. oyster sauce
1 tsp. sugar
¼ tsp. gourmet powder
1 Tbsp. dark soy
drops of sesame seed oil
⅓ C. water
1 ½ Tbsp. Wonder Powder
1 Tbsp. Chinese cooking wine

METHOD:

1) Marinate beef with 1 tsp. Wonder Powder, 2 Tbsp. light soy, 1 Tbsp. cooking wine and drops of sesame seed oil.
2) HEAT WOK*, brown green onion, garlic, onion and ginger. Add beef and saute until meat changes color. Add sauce and bring to a boil. Transfer to a heat-proof casserole.
3) Heat casserole until sauce comes to a boil. Serve from the casserole while sauce is still bubbling.

*refer HOW TO p. 21

BEEF

BEEF WITH MUSHROOMS

INGREDIENTS:

6 oz. beef steak, sliced
1 C. fresh mushrooms
1 C. straw mushrooms (canned)
8 Chinese mushrooms, soaked,
   cut in half
½ onion, wedged
1 green onion, cut to 1" lengths
½ tsp. minced garlic
½ tsp. minced ginger

SAUCE:

1 Tbsp. dark soy
1 tsp. sugar
2 Tbsp. oyster sauce
1 Tbsp. cooking wine
drops of sesame seed oil
dash pepper
½ C. water
1 Tbsp. Wonder Powder

METHOD:

1) Marinate beef with 1 Tbsp. Wonder Powder, 2 Tbsp. light soy, 1 Tbsp. cooking wine and drops of sesame seed oil.
2) HEAT WOK*, brown green onion, garlic and ginger; add beef and saute until meat changes color. Remove and set aside.
3) In same wok, STIR FRY* mushrooms and onion. Return beef to wok. Add sauce and cook until boils. Serve hot.

*refer HOW TO p. 21

PAPER WRAPPED BEEF

INGREDIENTS:

6 oz. beef steaks, sliced to ¼"
½ C. bamboo shoots
2 Tbsp. Chinese parsley (cut to
   2" lengths)
2 green onions, cut to 2" lengths
16 sheets, edible rice paper
   OR parchment paper*

SEASONING:

1 tsp. sugar
2 Tbsp. oyster sauce
½ tsp. Chinese 5 spice
1 Tbsp. cooking wine
drops of sesame seed oil
dash white pepper
1 Tbsp. Wonder Powder
1 Tbsp. water

BEEF

METHOD:

1) Marinate beef slices, bamboo shoots, Chinese parsley and green onions with all seasoning for 30 minutes.
2) Wrap 1 Tbsp. marinated beef in rice paper, folding up like an envelope, seal with egg.
3) DEEP FRY* at medium heat for 5-7 minutes. Drain and serve like an egg roll.

*NOTE: If parchment paper is used as substitute, you will have to open the paper packet to serve the beef.

*refer HOW TO p. 21

BEEF WITH CELLOPHANE NOODLES

INGREDIENTS:

12 oz. beef, sliced across
   grain to 1/3 thickness
1/2 tsp. minced garlic
1 tsp. minced ginger
1 sm. green pepper, shredded
1 sm. red pepper, shredded
2 oz. cellophane noodles,
2 oz. Bamboo shoots, sliced

SAUCE:

drops of sesame seed oil
1 Tbsp. light soy sauce
2 tsp. oyster sauce
1 tsp. sugar
1 tsp. Chinese cooking wine
1 1/2 Tbsp. Wonder Powder
1/2 C. water

METHOD:

1) Marinate beef with 1 Tbsp. YAN'S Wonder Powder, 2 Tbsp. light soy sauce, 1 tsp. sugar, dash pepper, 1/2 tsp. Chinese 5 spice powder and 1 tsp. Chinese cooking wine for half hour.
2) HEAT WOK*. When oil is very hot, drop in noodles. When they are "puffed up", remove with a wire ladle and spread on paper towel to drain. Place noodles on platter.
3) STIR FRY* all ingredients at high heat until beef changes color. Add sauce and bring to a boil. Pour over noodles.

*refer HOW TO p. 21

BEEF IN A NEST

INGREDIENTS:

14 oz. beef, sliced
1/3 C. water chestnuts
1/3 C. bamboo shoots
1/2 C. carrot, sliced
1/2 C. broccoli, flowerets
1/2 C. pineapple chunks, drained
1 small red pepper, wedged
1/2 tsp. minced garlic
1 tsp. minced ginger
*potatoes for making basket

SAUCE:

1 tsp. light soy
1 tsp. dark soy
1 Tbsp. oyster sauce
1 tsp. Chinese cooking wine
drops of sesame seed oil
1 Tbsp. Wonder Powder
1/4 C. water

METHOD:

1) Prepare basket*. (refer HOW TO p. 22)
2) Marinate beef with 1 Tbsp. Wonder Powder, 2 Tbsp. light soy, 1 tsp. Chinese cooking wine and drops of sesame seed oil.
3) HEAT WOK*, brown garlic, and ginger; put in beef and saute until meat changes color. Remove and set aside.
4) With same wok, add 1 Tbsp. peanut oil. STIR FRY* vegetables; return meat to wok. Add sauce and cook until boil, transfer to basket to serve.

*refer HOW TO p. 21

BEEF

BEEF WITH BABY CORN

INGREDIENTS:

8 oz. beef, sliced
1 C. baby corn
1 sm. carrot, sliced thinly
½ tsp. minced garlic
½ tsp. minced ginger
1 green onion, cut to 1" lengths

SAUCE:

1 tsp. sugar
¼ tsp. gourmet powder
drops sesame seed oil
dash pepper
1 Tbsp. Wonder Powder
¼ C. water

METHOD:

1) Marinate beef with 1 Tbsp. Wonder Powder, 2 tsp. light soy and 1 Tbsp. Chinese cooking wine.
2) Blanch baby corn in boiling water with ½ tsp. salt and 2 Tbsp. oil, drain and display on platter.
3) HEAT WOK*, brown green onion, garlic and ginger, put in beef and carrot; saute for 1 minute. Add sauce and bring to boil. Pour on top of baby corn and serve hot.

*refer HOW TO p. 21

BEEF WITH POTATO

INGREDIENTS:

10 oz. beef slices
6 oz. potato, slivered
then soak in water for ½ hour
1 green onion, cut to 1"
½ tsp. garlic, minced
½ tsp. ginger, minced

SAUCE:

1 Tbsp. dark soy
1 Tbsp. oyster sauce
1 Tbsp. light soy
½ tsp. sugar
drops sesame seed oil
1 tsp. Chinese cooking wine
1/3 C. water
1 Tbsp. Wonder Powder

METHOD:

1) Marinate beef with 1 tsp. Wonder Powder, 2 tsp. light soy, 1 tsp. cooking wine, and drops of sesame seed oil.
2) Heat oil, DEEP FRY* potato chips and display in a platter.
3) HEAT WOK*, brown green onion, garlic and ginger; put in beef and saute until meat changes color. Add sauce and cook until boiling. Pour over potato chips to serve.

*refer HOW TO p. 21

BEEF

CURRIED BEEF SKEWER

INGREDIENTS:

1 lb. beef flank steaks
  (cut across grain 1" thickness
  in 4" strips, scored in middle
  of one side)
12 bamboo skewers 8" long
½ tsp. minced ginger
¼ tsp. minced garlic
1 small onion, shredded

SAUCE:

½ C. cream
¼ tsp. gourmet powder
1 Tbsp. Chinese cooking wine
2 Tbsp. Wonder Powder to
  ¼ C. water
¾ tsp. salt
dash pepper
1 tsp. sugar
3 Tbsp. curry powder

METHOD:

1) Using a meat tenderizer, hammer beef; marinate with 2 Tbsp. dark soy, 1 egg, Chinese cooking wine, salt, pepper and 2 Tbsp. Wonder Powder for ½ hour. Put on beef skewers.
2) DEEP FRY* BEEF for 5 minutes. Remove, drain oil.
3) HEAT WOK*. Saute ginger, garlic and onion ½ minute. Add sauce and bring to a boil. Pour over beef skewers.

*refer HOW TO p. 21

BEEF WITH BEAN SPROUTS

INGREDIENTS:

8 oz. beef, sliced across grain
1 lb. bean sprouts
¼ C. carrots, shredded
¼ C. celery, shredded
1 sm. green pepper, shredded
½ tsp. minced ginger
½ tsp. minced garlic
1 stalk green onion, cut to
  1" lengths

SAUCE:

1 tsp. sugar
1 Tbsp. light soy sauce
1 Tbsp. oyster sauce
½ tsp. salt
1 tsp. Chinese cooking wine
drops of sesame seed oil
1 Tbsp. Wonder Powder
¼ C. water

METHOD:

1) Marinate beef with 2 Tbsp. light soy sauce and 1 Tbsp. Wonder Powder for 5 to 10 minutes.
2) HEAT WOK*, add ginger, garlic and onion and stir for half minute. Add beef and stir until meat changes color. Remove and set aside.
3) Add all vegetables and STIR FRY*.
4) Return beef to wok, add sauce, bring to a boil and mix well.

*refer HOW TO p. 21

PRAWNS CHOW MEIN

INGREDIENTS:

10 oz. fresh noodles
20 prawns, deveined
1 C. bok choy OR broccoli
    cut to 2" lengths
1 stalk green onion, cut to
    1" lengths
½ tsp. minced garlic
¼ tsp. minced ginger

SAUCE:

1 tsp. salt
1 tsp. sugar
½ tsp. gourmet powder
1 Tbsp. Chinese cooking wine
½ C. water
1 ½ Tbsp. Wonder Powder
drops of sesame seed oil

METHOD:

1) Dry prawns with paper towel. Marinate with ½ tsp. salt, ½ tsp. sugar, 1 tsp. Wonder Powder and drops of sesame seed oil.
2) Blanch noodles for ½ minute. Drain and cool in collander for half hour.
3) HEAT WOK*, brown noodles on both sides and transfer to platter.
4) HEAT WOK*, saute green onions, garlic and ginger for a few seconds. Add prawns and saute for 1 minute. Remove and set aside.
5) STIR FRY* vegetables, return prawns, add sauce and bring to a boil. Pour over bed of noodles.

*refer HOW TO p. 21

PORK CHOW MEIN

INGREDIENTS:

10 oz. fresh noodles
8 oz. lean pork, shredded
4 Chinese mushrooms, soaked
    and shredded
1 C. bean sprouts
3 stalks green onion, cut to
    2" lengths

SAUCE:

¹/₂ tsp. salt
1 tsp. sugar
2 Tsp. oyster sauce
1 Tbsp. dark soy sauce
1 Tbsp. Chinese cooking wine
1 ½ Tbsp. Wonder Powder
½ C. water
drops of sesame seed oil

METHOD:

1) Blanch noodles for ½ minute. Drain in collander for half hour.
2) Marinate pork with 1 tsp. Wonder Powder, 1 Tbsp. light soy sauce, 1 tsp. Chinese cooking wine and drops of sesame seed oil.
3) HEAT WOK*, brown noodles on both sides and transfer to platter.
4) HEAT WOK*, saute pork for 1 minute. Add Chinese mushrooms, bean sprouts and cook another minute. Add sauce and bring to boil. Pour over bed of noodles on platter.

*refer HOW TO p. 21

MISCELLANEOUS

99

MINCED BEEF FRIED RICE

INGREDIENTS:

¾ C. ground beef
¼ C. chopped onion
¼ C. frozen green peas
3 C. cooked rice
1 egg, beaten
1 stalk green onion, chopped

SEASONING:

1 tsp. salt
1 tsp. sugar
¼ tsp. gourmet powder
1 Tbsp. dark soy sauce

METHOD:

1) Marinate beef with 1 tsp. Wonder Powder, 1 Tbsp. light soy sauce, 1 tsp. Chinese cooking wine and drops of sesame seed oil.
2) HEAT WOK*, saute onions, ground beef and loosen meat with spatula. Cook until meat changes color. Add cooked rice and egg. Mix well.
3) Add seasoning, green onions and green peas. Use medium heat to fry the rice until hot.

*refer HOW TO p. 21

BEEF AND TOMATO CHOW MEIN

INGREDIENTS:

10 oz. fresh noodles
8 oz. beef, sliced
2 tomatoes, wedged
½ onion, wedged
½ tsp. minced garlic

SAUCE:

½ tsp. salt
3 Tbsp. sugar
1 Tbsp. vinegar
¼ C. tomato ketchup
½ C. water
2 Tbsp. Wonder Powder

METHOD:

1) Marinate beef with 1 tsp. Wonder Powder, 1 Tbsp. light soy sauce, drops of sesame seed oil and 1 Tbsp. Chinese cooking wine.
2) Blanch noodles for ½ minute. Drain in collander and let cool.
3) HEAT WOK*, brown noodles on both sides. Transfer to platter.
4) Clean and HEAT WOK*, brown garlic for a few seconds. Saute onion and beef until meat changes color. Add sauce, bring to boil and pour over noodles.

*refer HOW TO p. 21

HONEYMOON FRIED RICE

INGREDIENTS:

3 C. cooked rice

A) 8 oz. chicken meat, sliced
¼ C. frozen peas
1 egg white, beaten

B) 8 oz. beef, sliced
½ onion, cut into 6 wedges

SAUCE:

A) For Chicken:

½ tsp. salt
½ tsp. sugar
¼ tsp. gourmet powder
1 tsp. cooking wine
drops sesame seed oil
½ C. water
1 ½ Tbsp. Wonder Powder

B) For Beef:

½ tsp. salt
3 Tbsp. sugar
2 Tbsp. tomato paste
1 Tbsp. vinegar
½ C. water
1 ½ Tbsp. Wonder Powder

METHOD:

1) Marinate chicken with ½ tsp. salt, 1 tsp. Wonder Powder, 1 tsp. Chinese cooking wine and drops of sesame seed oil.
2) Marinate beef with 1 tsp. Wonder Powder, 1 Tbsp. light soy sauce, 1 Tbsp. Chinese cooking wine and drops of sesame seed oil.
3) STIR FRY* cooked rice in wok, sprinkle ½ tsp. salt. Use medium heat and cook rice until hot. Transfer to a casserole dish. Clean wok.
4) HEAT WOK* saute chicken until meat changes color. Add chicken sauce and bring to boil. Stir in egg white. Pour over one side of rice.
5) Clean and HEAT WOK*. Saute onion for half minute and add beef. Stir until meat changes color. Add beef sauce and bring to boil. Pour over other side of the rice.

*refer HOW TO p. 21

MISCELLANEOUS

PINEAPPLE FRIED RICE

INGREDIENTS:

1 pineapple with leaves
  cut in half lengthwise
  (hollow one half)
½ C. pineapple, chopped fine
2 C. cooked rice
1/3 C. cooked ham (diced)
1 egg, beaten
1/3 C. frozen peas
1 green onion, chopped

SEASONING:

1 ½ tsp. light soy
½ tsp. salt

METHOD:

1) HEAT WOK*, fry beaten egg and scramble with spatula into small pieces. Add rest of ingredients except hollowed half of pineapple to the seasoning, saute at medium heat until rice is heated up. Transfer to hollow pineapple to serve.

*refer HOW TO p. 21

RICE NOODLES WITH BEEF

INGREDIENTS:

3 C. rice noodles, softened
1 C. beef slices
3 green onion, cut to 2"
½ small onion, shredded
1 C. bean sprouts
1 tsp. ginger, finely shredded

SEASONING:

½ tsp. salt
½ tsp. sugar
2 Tbsp. dark soy sauce
dash pepper
drops of sesame seed oil

METHOD:

1) Marinate beef with ½ tsp. Wonder Powder, 1 Tbsp. light soy, 1 tsp. cooking wine and drops sesame seed oil.
2) HEAT WOK*, brown green onion, shredded onion and ginger; put in beef and saute until meat changes color. Remove and set aside.
3) With same wok, add 2 Tbsp. peanut oil, saute bean sprouts for 2 minutes. Add rice noodles, saute for another 2 minutes. Return meat to wok, add seasoning. Mix well.

*refer HOW TO p. 21

MISCELLANEOUS

YAN'S HOT NOODLES

INGREDIENTS:

10 oz. fresh noodles
¼ C. shrimp, cooked
¼ C. ham, cooked and shredded
2 eggs, beaten
½ C. celery, shredded
1 green pepper (small) shredded
1 carrot (small) shredded
½ onion, shredded
2 Tbsp. curry powder

SEASONING:

½ tsp. salt
1 tsp. sugar
½ tsp. gourmet powder
2 Tbsp. water
1 Tbsp. light soy sauce
1 Tbsp. oyster sauce

METHOD:

1) Blanch noodles for ½ minute and drain in collander for half hour.
2) Smear 1 tsp. peanut oil on the surface of the wok. Use medium heat to cook egg as to form an egg sheet. Remove and cut into strips.
3) HEAT WOK*, saute vegetables and curry powder for ½ minute. Then add meat and saute for another ½ minute. Add seasoning, noodles and egg strips. Stir mix well.

*refer HOW TO p. 21

HAM FRIED RICE

INGREDIENTS:

4-6 C. Cooked rice, cold
1-2 C. Diced Ham
3 Tbsp. dark soy sauce
2 eggs, large, beaten with dash of salt
1 tsp. Chinese cooking wine
2-3 stalks green onion, chopped fine
1 C. frozen green peas, thawed

METHOD:

1) Use medium heat and 3 Tbsp. of peanut oil, fry meat for 2 minutes.
2) Add rice and stir with a spatula constantly for 3-5 minutes until the rice is hot.
3) Sprinkle wine, and then add ½ tsp. of salt, dark soy sauce and green peas.
4) Gently and slowly pour the beaten eggs over the rice. Turn the rice with a spatula constantly until the eggs become solid.
5) Sprinkle with green onions, mix and serve hot.

MISCELLANEOUS

LONG LIFE BUN

INGREDIENTS:

8 oz. flour
8 oz. frozen bread dough
3 oz. sugar
1 Tbsp. shortening
½ tsp. ammonium carbonate
¼ tsp. lye water
2 Tbsp. water
1 tsp. vinegar
1 tsp. baking powder

FOR FILLING:

½ lb. mashed sweet lotus seed
OR mashed sweet bean paste.
(Available in Chinatown)

METHOD:

1) Thaw bread dough in a bowl with ½ C. warm water, cover with a damp towel, let rise in warm place for 2 hours or until double in size.

2) Mix sugar, ammonium carbonate powder, vinegar and water with 8 oz. flour.

3) Add lye water and shortening to bread dough. Knead well and mix with flour dough. Cover with a damp towel and let rise for 15 minutes.

4) Knead lightly and let stand for a few more minutes. Repeat procedure once more.

5) Shape dough into long roll and divide into 12 pieces. Press with hand to give 3" round shapes. Add 1 Tbsp. of filling. Wrap by gathering edge and twisting to a sharp point on top. Use a small knife to make an indentation line from the sharp point to bottom. Place on small piece of waxed paper and let rise for 10 minutes.

6) Steam at high heat for 8 minutes. When done, dab lightly with red food coloring along indentation line. Makes 12.

TO: "WOK WITH YAN"

To "wok" with you every day
Is very helpful in every way.
For half an hour nothing gets done,
But really; I do enjoy the fun.
Each day I look forward to you;
To hear & see the things you do.
Yes; you are extremely good.
To "wok" with you; anyone would.

C. Carson, Seattle Washington, U.S.A.

MISCELLANEOUS

BARBEQUED PORK BUN

INGREDIENTS:

8 oz. flour
8 oz. frozen bread dough
3 oz. sugar
1 Tbsp. shortening
½ tsp. ammonium carbonate
¼ tsp. lye water
1 tsp. vinegar
1 tsp. baking powder

FILLING:

8 oz. BBQ pork, diced
½ tsp. minced garlic
1 Tbsp. green onion, chopped
½ tsp. minced ginger

FOR SAUCE:

1 Tbsp. oyster sauce
2 tsp. light soy sauce
3 Tbsp. sugar
1 Tbsp. dark soy sauce
dash pepper
drops sesame seed oil
$^1/_3$ C. water
2 Tbsp. Wonder Powder

METHOD:

1) Thaw bread dough in a bowl with ½ C. warm water, cover with a damp towel and let rise in warm place for 2 hours or until double in size.

2) Mix sugar, ammonium carbonate powder, vinegar and water with 8 oz. flour.

3) Add lye water and shortening to the bread dough. Knead well and mix with flour dough. Cover with a damp towel and let rise for 15 minutes.

4) Knead lightly and let stand for a few more minutes. Repeat procedure once more.

5) HEAT WOK*, brown garlic, ginger and onions. Add sauce mixture and cook until boiling. Add BBQ pork. Mix well. Remove and chill in refrigerator for 1 hour.

6) Shape dough into long roll and divide into 12 pieces. Press with hand to give 3" round shape. Add 1 Tbsp. filling. Wrap up by gathering edges and twisting on top to close. Place bun on small piece of waxed paper. Let stand for 10 minutes.

7) Steam at high heat for 10 minutes. Makes 12.

*refer HOW TO p. 21

MISCELLANEOUS

GUM LOW WON TON

FOR GUM LOW:

4 pcs. BBQ pork
4 pcs. cooked ham
4 pcs. cooked chicken
4 prawns
½ onion, wedged
½ green pepper, wedged
½ red pepper, wedged
1 tomato, wedged
½ tsp. minced garlic

FOR WON TON:

INGREDIENTS:

16 won ton wrappers
½ C. ground pork
¼ C. shrimp, diced

SAUCE:

1/3 C. vinegar
1/3 C. water
1/3 C. sugar
½ tsp. salt
1 ½ Tbsp. Wonder Powder
2 Tbsp. tomato paste

METHOD:

1) Mix pork, shrimp with ½ tsp. salt. Place ½ tsp. of mixture on 1 piece of wrapper. Wrap as won ton. Repeat procedure until all wrappers are used up.
2) DEEP FRY* until golden brown. Arrange on platter and clean wok.
3) HEAT WOK*, saute garlic, onion, peppers, prawns and tomato. Add sauce and all other ingredients and bring to a boil. Pour over won tons and serve immediately.
*refer HOW TO p. 21

SIU MAI

INGREDIENTS:

1 ½ C. minced pork
4 Chinese mushrooms (soaked and minced)
¼ C. bamboo shoots, minced
1 egg yolk
30 won ton skins

SEASONING:

1 tsp. salt
1 tsp. sugar
½ tsp. gourmet powder
drops sesame seed oil
1 tsp. Chinese cooking wine
1 ½ Tbsp. Wonder Powder

METHOD:

1) Marinate pork with seasoning for 15 minutes.
2) Mix in all other ingredients. Knead well.
3) Trim won ton skins into round circles.
4) Place 1 Tbsp. of filling into center of won ton skin. Take skin between index finger & thumb to form a waist. Use a wet spoon to press filling down so that it is compact and has a smooth top.
5) Oil steamer and steam Siu Mai for 10 to 15 minutes at high heat.
*refer HOW TO p. 21

106

GOLDEN FRIED DUMPLING

FILLING:

2 C. ground pork
¼ C. green onions, minced
½ C. bamboo shoots, minced
2 Tbsp. minced ginger

WRAPPER:

3 C. flour
1 C. hot water
3 Tbsp. cold water

SEASONING:

2 tsp. salt
2 tsp. sugar
½ tsp. gourmet powder
2 Tbsp. wonder powder
1 Tbsp. Chinese cooking wine
1 Tbsp. sesame seed oil
dash pepper

METHOD:

1) Mix filling ingredients together with seasoning and marinate for ½ hour. Chill in refrigerator.
2) Pour hot water in flour and add cold water. Knead well and let stand for 10 minutes.
3) Make a long roll and cut into 36 pieces and roll into 2" round wrapper.
4) Place 1 Tbsp. of filling in the middle of each wrapper. Fold in half and pinch edge to seal.
5) HEAT WOK*. Place dumplings close together in wok so that they form a tight circle. Cook for 2 minutes to brown the bottom of dumplings. Add ½ C. water, cover and let cook until water dries up (about 4 mins.). Remove wok lid, shake wok, or use spatula to loosen dumplings so that dumplings do not stick. Cook until golden brown on bottom only.
6) Transfer to platter with golden brown side on top. Serve with vinegar, soy sauce and shredded ginger to taste.

*refer HOW TO p. 21

MISCELLANEOUS

4 FLAVOURED DUMPLINGS

INGREDIENTS:

FOR FILLING:

2 C. shrimp, diced
¼ C. bamboo shoots, minced
1 Tbsp. green onions, minced
½ tsp. minced ginger
1 tsp. salt
1 tsp. sugar
½ tsp. gourmet powder
drops of sesame seed oil
1 tsp. Chinese cooking wine
dash pepper
1 Tbsp. Wonder Powder

FOR SKIN:

2½ C. flour
¾ C. boiling water
¼ tsp. salt
1 Tbsp. shortening

4 FLAVOURS FOR SEASONING:

2 Tbsp. cooked ham, minced
2 Tbsp. green onions, minced
2 Tbsp. tomato, chopped fine
2 Tbsp. boiled egg yolk, mashed

METHOD:

1) Mix all "filling" ingredients together and knead well. Chill in refrigerator.
2) Make dough by pouring boiling water in flour. Add salt and shortening. Knead well and let stand for 15 minutes.
3) Make a long roll and cut into 30 small pieces and roll out into 2" round skins with rolling pin. Put 1 Tbsp. filling in middle of each skin. Gather 2 opposite edges together and pinch to stick at middle point. Repeat procedure for opposite side to form a dumpling with 4 openings.
4) Put different flavours "for seasoning" into each of the 4 openings.
5) Oil steamer and steam for 5 minutes at high heat.

Every day at half past twelve
We turn our T.V. on
To watch that little Chinese guy
Put his Wok show on.

He kids around an awful lot
and the audience seem to love it
If they ever took him off the air
We'd miss him quite a bit.

So here's to the cook they call Stephen Yan
Who's never seen to use a garbage can
Whatever you do, don't ever stop
And you'll always be "Cock of the Wok".

M. Scofield, Vancouver, B.C., Canada

CHINESE SHRIMP BUN

INGREDIENTS:

3 C. flour
1-1 ½ C. water

FOR FILLING:

1 C. shrimp, minced
½ onion, chopped
¼ C. cooked ham, minced
1 green onion, minced
½ tsp. minced ginger

SEASONING:

½ tsp. salt
½ tsp. sugar
¼ tsp. gourmet powder
dash pepper
drops of sesame seed oil
1 Tbsp. Wonder Powder

METHOD:

1) Mix flour and water to make dough. Knead well and divide into 30 portions. Roll out into circular sheets about 2½" in diameter.
2) HEAT WOK*, brown green onion and ginger. Add shrimp, onion and saute for ½ minute. Add seasoning and cook for another minute. Remove to platter and cool.
3) Place 1 Tbsp. filling in middle of wrapper. Place another wrapper on top of filling. Seal by pressing down and pinching the edges.
4) DEEP FRY* until golden brown.

*refer HOW TO p. 21

CURRIED BEEF TRIANGLES

INGREDIENTS:

1 C. minced beef
small onion, chopped
6 spring roll wrappers

SEASONING:

2 tsp. curry powder
½ tsp. salt
½ tsp. sugar
1 tsp. light soy sauce
1 tsp. YAN'S Wonder Powder
¼ tsp. 5 spice powder

METHOD:

1) Marinate beef and onion with all seasonings.
2) HEAT WOK*, saute beef for 5 minutes. Remove and set aside.
3) Cut wrapper into strips of 2" wide. Form a triangle on one end and put in 1 Tbsp. beef mixture and roll up with the remaining wrapper, seal the end with beaten egg.
4) DEEP FRY*

*refer HOW TO p. 21

MISCELLANEOUS

SPONGE CAKE

INGREDIENTS:

1 C. flour
½ C. sugar
3 eggs, beaten
½ tsp. baking soda

1 tsp. vanilla extract
4 Tbsp. margarine, melted
½ C. evaporated milk
1 tsp. baking powder

METHOD:

1) Put all ingredients in a large bowl and beat well for 5 minutes.
2) Pour mixture into large greased pan and steam at high heat for 25 minutes.
3) When done, remove and slice.

SHRIMP DUMPLINGS

INGREDIENTS:
FOR FILLING:

2 C. raw shrimp, diced
½ C. bamboo shoots, minced
1 oz. pork fat, minced

FOR SKINS:

3 Tbsp. Wonder Powder
1½ C. non-glutinous flour OR
   potato flour
1½ C. boiling water
1 Tbsp. vegetable shortening

SEASONING:

1 tsp. salt
½ tsp. gourmet powder
1 tsp. sugar
dash pepper
1 tsp. sesame seed oil
½ egg white
1 Tbsp. Wonder Powder

METHOD:

1) Marinate shrimp with seasoning for 20 minutes. Add bamboo shoots and pork fat. Stir mix in a circular motion for 3 mins. Chill in refrigerator.
2) Make dough by pouring boiling water in the non-glutinous flour, add shortening and knead until smooth.
3) Make a long roll and cut into 30 small portions. Roll each into a 2" round shape. Put 1 Tbsp. filling in the middle of each skin. Fold in half and pinch edge to seal.
4) Place in oiled steamer. Use high heat and steam for 5 minutes. Makes 30 pieces.

MONGOLIAN FIREPOT

INGREDIENTS:

½ C. beef, sliced
½ C. chicken meat, sliced
½ C. pork, sliced
½ C. scallops, cut in half
½ C. fish filet, sliced
½ C. prawns, sliced
3 C. spinach
2 C. swiss chard, cut to 2" lengths
1 C. cellophane noodles, soaked
1 C. bean curd, cut in
rectangular pieces

SOUP:

6 C. water
1 cube chicken boullion
1 tsp. salt
1 tsp. sugar
1 tsp. cooking wine
drops sesame seed oil
¼ tsp. gourmet powder

SAUCE MIX:

½ C. dark soy
¼ C. cooking oil, heated
2 green onion, minced
2 eggs, beaten

METHOD:

1) Marinate meats separately each with 2 Tbsp. light soy, dash of pepper, drops of sesame seed oil and 1 Tbsp. cooking oil.
2) Marinate seafood separately each with ½ tsp. salt, dash of pepper, drops of sesame seed oil and 1 Tbsp. cooking oil.
3) Arrange all ingredients on small plate.
4) Bring soup into a boil and pour to the firepot, if not available, use a deep fryer.
5) Cook meat, seafood or vegetable in hot soup in a small basket. When done, remove and dip in sauce to serve.

ALMOND COOKIES

INGREDIENTS:

10 oz. flour
¼ tsp. baking powder
¼ tsp. ammonium carbonate
blanched almonds

4 oz. shortening (lard)
2 eggs
6 oz. sugar

METHOD:

1) Mix baking powder and flour and sift on top of a tray. Put in sugar, ammonium carbonate powder, melted shortening and 1 egg. Knead well.
2) Pre-heat oven to 250°F. Knead flour mixture into a roll. Divide roll into approximately 30-35 portions. Flatten each portion with a rolling pin to make a round shape. Place on a greased pan in the centre of each, make a dent and then place the almond on top.
3) Brush egg mixture on top of cookie and then bake in oven at 250°F for 10 minutes. Then increase to 300°F and bake another 10 minutes until golden brown.

HOW DO YOU LIKE IT!

"...You seem to make everything so easy, I think that your show is the only one that makes me hungry"...

C. Rurredge, Powell River, B.C., Canada

"...I watch your show so often that I am becoming a wok-a-holic.."

L. McCarthy, Burlington, VT. U.S.A.

"...I enjoy your shows immensely and find all the dishes delicious looking I want to "Wok with Yan" therefore I would appreciate it, if you would kindly send me your cookbook, so I can be the "headwoker" of them all".

J. Lonno, Montreal, Quebec, Canada

"...There are no words to express how much joy and help we get from your program"...

E. Spurrer, Marysville, Wa. U.S.A.

"...I enjoy your ideas and methods, it's a pleasure to pick up tips from a Chinese cross between Johnny Carson and the Galloping Gourmet"...

B. Moore, Winnipeg, Manitoba, Canada

"...My mother says, you cook like a professional chef, but your jokes are cornier than that of Benny Hill"

M. Reimer, Lethbridge, Alberta, Canada

"...Out of all the Chinese cooking shows I have watched, your's is by far the best, besides being handy with a wok you have a good sense of humor..."

J. Winter, Calgary, Alberta Canada

"...Your T.V. Show is very good, your dishes look fantastic, and your humor picks up my morning."

J. Davis, Norwalk, Ohio U.S.A.

"...Thank you for your cheerful morning T.V. Show..you do it with very good taste..your humor is done very well and don't ever give it up..."

A. Mastro, Brandon, Manitoba, Canada

"...My son who is 2½ yrs. old, doesn't miss your show ever since he's seen the one with popcorn popping all over the place..."

R. Chasse, Kelowna, B.C. Canada

"...Mr. Yan, your jokes are very good even kids enjoy your program..."

M. Coresa, Edmonton, Alberta Canada

"...A short while ago, I had the privilege of viewing your show while visiting in Michigan. I was thrilled to be able to come back home with about seven of your recipes..."

J. Flowers, Fresno, California U.S.A.

"...I'm 64 years old, I have made some of your delicious recipes, even my 13 year old granddaughter has learned to cook by watching you."

Mrs. M. Marranca, Surrey, B.C. Canada

"...caught your program for the first time, 5 or 6 weeks ago, and have become hopelessly addicted..."

S. Landreth, Cranbrook, B.C., Canada